Tickle Me With Love

Ricki McCallum

Tickle Me With Love

Christian Poems & Short Stories

Ricki McCallum

Ricki McCallum Books

Finally A Broker!
Open Your Own Real Estate Office

Downsizing Homes
What You Need to Know

Pandemic Real Estate
Buyers, Seller, & Realtors®

Buying Your First Home
A Step-by-Step Guide from Dreams to Reality

Dingle Doo
Little Brother from Hell

Heart Calls
Christian Poems, Prayers, & Short Stories

Snow Fire
Murder, Suspense, & Intrigue

Snow Fire 2
Revenge & Justice

Dedication

To all the positive people in my life

who are always spreading joy

and making others laugh.

(You know who you are)

Proverbs 17:22 KJV

A merry heart doeth good like a medicine:

but a broken spirit drieth the bones.

Table of Contents

Poems Italicized *

Introduction

Introduction

TICKLE ME WITH LOVE begins with a poem and the Aurora Borealis story. Then, comes the stories of Mason, a lonely, depressed widower. After a heart transformation, his whole life changes.

Summer Fun is the second poem and *"every poem is italicized"* in the table of contents. You will find humor in many of them like in Author to Author and Irresistible Cheese.

Relive your childhood fantasies in Chapter 2 with stories like Imaginations of a Garment Thief. A Woman's Voice speaks loudly in Chapter 3 with The Birthday Dinner, Crazy Mary, and Chicken Pot Pie.

Christmas stories will touch your heart in Chapter 4, and Chapter 5 is all about Cousin Annie. Folks think she talks a little funny, but it's just her neck of the woods talkin'. Annie is a very smart woman if you count common sense, hard work, rearing children, and being resourceful as attributes of good thinking and higher understanding. Down south in the 1980's is the setting for her stories.

Chapter 6 starts with a poem, Danger, Danger Everywhere, but the danger stories have a great ending. Chapter 7 gives a Manly Point of View. Humor abounds in some of the stories, and your heart gets touched in a special way.

Chapter 8 will appeal to everyone with heart-warming and funny stories. Good Decisions describes Chapter 9 and ends with three poems and a letter to my readers.

So, get ready to read one story at a time or the whole book. Each story will lift you up and give you a happy feeling inside. This book should put a smile on your face many times over. Poems are scattered throughout the chapters.

Taken in Effingham, Illinois

Chapter 1
Praise The Lord

Tickle Me With Love

I searched and searched for the perfect name,
Stories and poems like Heart Calls; not the same.
More humor and fun are found in all of these,
In Heart Calls, high emotion was the key.

Tickle Me With Love shows God's humor with care,
Laughter and merriment should fill the air.
God loves a good laugh or two or three,
The stories and poems just came to me.

I am just the writer of many of His tales,
Putting my fingers on keys they begin to sail.
I know it is the Lord writing these things,
Joy and peace, His stories always bring.

I am Tickled by His Love, as I write,
Words come by faith and not by sight.
I hear His voice, oh so well,
When in His Holy presence, I dwell.

The Aurora Borealis

Kathy came running inside from the backyard. "Mom, come look! The Northern Lights are beautiful!"

I immediately stopped washing the dinner dishes and went outside with my little girl. She was right. The Aurora Borealis tonight was spectacular. It never gets old looking at them. Some nights are better than others, but here in the Upper Peninsula of Michigan, the lights are often seen.

I stood there looking up, observing the green and blue curtains of lights. Then, I saw to the right near the horizon a shade of red ribbons. "Mom, see the red ones?"

"Yes, honey. I see them."

"Old Buckey says the earth is angry when we see the red ones."

"Is that right? What else does old Buckey, the Indian at the museum, say? Did he say it is time for you to be in bed?" I laughed.

"Mom, he said the wolves are out at night when you see the red ones."

"Really? We should go see Old Buckey tomorrow

and see what else he has to say."

"Oh, Mom. That's a great idea. I have two quarters I saved from lunch today."

"Good, we can use those."

I knew Kathy would have a hard time sleeping tonight. She loved going to the museum, and I liked it too. It would be nice to go again tomorrow.

Old Buckey was a wooden Indian that stood near the front door of the museum. When someone placed a quarter in his hand, the hand would rotate and drop the quarter into his pocket. Then Old Buckey, the wonderful storyteller, would tell a tale. Old Buckey's tales always mesmerized the children that visited the museum.

This week's tales were again about the Aurora Borealis, and I thought, what a great time to visit the museum. I could teach my little girl more about the Northern Lights that fascinated her so much.

The museum had few visitors after school, and we went straight to Old Buckey the next day. There he stood, brown-toned skin in authentic buckskin clothes and feathers in his hair. He was six feet tall, and his features were lifelike. People often took him for a real man when they first saw him. He was a treasure to our little museum.

"Here's my quarters, mom. Put one in."

I put a quarter in Old Buckey's hand and it rotated and dropped the quarter into his pocket. Old Buckey came alive and began to talk. Kathy was smiling and listening closely. She didn't want to miss a word Old Buckey said. Kathy practically memorized his stories. She loved repeating them to me.

The Northern Lights, he began, were placed there by request from an Indian princess. She was waiting for her groom. His hunting party had been delayed, and she was anxiously awaiting his return. She watched and waited for many days, but he never came back. The tribe told her to forget about him. He would never return.

The Indian princess cried and cried. She said she could not live without her young hunter. The other people tried to console her, but she said she would never stop waiting for him. She placed lights in her house and along the paths that lead to their camp. She wanted him to see his way home. When he still did not come, she prayed to the Great Spirit.

The Great Spirit placed beautiful colored lights in the sky. Colors of green, blue, red, and orange. The young man could surely see his way home now. The strong and proud young hunter never came.

The princess eventually left to go home to the Great Spirit, and her young hunter met her there. Today, they dance a beautiful waltz among the lights in the sky. Old Buckey said to watch the lights as they move from side to side and up and down. You may see the young princess and her hunter.

"Wow, Mom. Tonight, we will watch and maybe we will see her."

I patted Kathy on the head, and we left the museum. It was a good story Old Buckey told, but now I was curious. What are the Northern Lights? I've looked at them for years and admired their beauty, but I know so little about them.

I googled more information about the Northern Lights or Aurora Borealis. I found there are also Southern Lights. They are caused by solar wind disturbances in the magnetosphere. It is the speed and projections of solar particles that are in the upper regions of our atmosphere near the Arctic and the Antarctic. It was over my head, but basically it is like a windstorm from the sun.

Whatever it is, it is beautiful and I know our God, the Great Spirit, to some, put them there for our enjoyment. Beautiful colors in the sky that dance. We are so blessed to live in the far north. These remarkable signs in the sky are often seen.

Infinite Love

My God is delicate as a flower,
Yet He is as big as the sky.
If you don't believe me,
Just look at the Northern Lights.

Sweet roses smell so good,
They intoxicate the air.
God knows us very well,
Even the numbers of our hair.

How can I show Him,
How much I love Him so?
My heart daily rejoices,
In Love He constantly shows.

Dear sweet Lord of mine,
How much sweeter each day.
My mind cannot comprehend,
When in spirit, at your feet, I lay.

The Holy Spirit takes me to new places.
I drown in your infinite love.
Nothing is better than the riches,
That come from heaven above.

Oh, Lord, I want to sing and praise,
All day long and into the night.
May my joy be everlasting,
As I cling to you, with all my might.

Praise the Lord

♪♫ *Praising the Lord! Praise the Lord!* ♪♫

I hear the enthusiastic melody coming from the little white wooden church that sits on the meadow. The little church was built by pioneers many decades ago, but it is still open, and people in these parts are still there every Sunday morning praising and worshipping the Lord.

It does my heart good to know some things never change. In a world of modern conveniences, trying times, simple goodness is cherished. People who truly believe in the Lord and take time out of their busy schedules to go and sing,
and read the Bible together touch me. I wish I had the same beliefs. I might not feel so empty if I thought there was a God out there that truly cared about me. If I thought the end of this life would bring justice and mercy and a better afterlife, my decisions today and tomorrow would be different.

I go about my daily business on Sunday, just like any

other day. People don't mind these days. Back in the 1960s, I would be frowned upon for working on Sunday, but not today. Everything is accepted today.

I mow my lawn and then sit on the porch with a glass of iced tea. I watch as the people leave the church. They shake hands and hug one another. I wonder do they really like each other that much, or is it just on Sunday?

I put my iced tea down on the table by my chair and get up to go turn off
the sprinkler. I like to water the lawn after I mow, but it's had enough water now. Walking down the porch steps, my foot got tangled in the water hose and I tripped. I fell three steps down onto the cement sidewalk. No biggie. I tried to get up, but realized I turned my ankle and it was already swelling.

"Ouch!" I hollered.

A couple across the way on the church parking lot saw what happened and ran over to see if they could help me.

"Are you okay?" the man asked.

The lady saw my ankle swelling and gasped. I looked down and I saw some blood. I knew this was worse than I thought. The man reached down to help pick me up. I held my ankle off the ground and tried to get my balance. He put his arm under my arm to relieve the weight of my own body on my leg.

"Thank you, thank you," I said.

Feeling helpless is not something I am used to and I don't like it. That's when
everything went dark. I awoke in the emergency room at the hospital. There was a bright light shining in my eyes, and doctors and nurses were all around the table.

"What happened?"

The doctor spoke. "We're not sure yet. We are running tests to see why you passed out."

"How'd I get here?"

"A young couple brought you in. They said they saw you fall and went to help and that is when you passed out. They brought you to the hospital. Who are they?"

"I don't know. They go to the church across the street from my house."

"Well, we are going to fix your ankle and you'll be able to leave before too long if nothing else is found wrong with you. Okay?"

"Sure, Doc. Sounds great to me. I don't like hospitals."

It was a funny thing. I passed out from shock. My ankle was broken, and it was a pretty bad break. The doctor had to pin it and put a cast on. I never dreamed such a simple accident could do so much damage. Here I am, laid up in my house now for weeks.

The nice couple are Dan and Sherry Brooks. They told me they have lived in this community their entire lives. I didn't know them before. Of course, I don't get out and mingle with people. I am a homebody. I enjoy staying to myself. No neighbors out here in the country, except for the church across the street. I rarely see anybody. Since I retired, going to town to shop is my only outing most weeks. I like being solitary.

"Knock, knock," Sherry calls from the front door.

"Come on in," I yell back.

"I'm bringing you some homemade chicken and dumplings today with a fresh garden salad. Mrs. Cutter made the chicken and dumplings, but the salad is from me. I grew those tomatoes and leaf lettuce in my garden."

"Sherry, that is very nice of you, but you and the church people don't have to
do this for me."

"Oh, but we want to," she said.

I am not used to being around people, and having them help me feels awkward.

"Now you just get well."

She comes over and props up my pillows.

"You don't need to help me. I can take care of myself."

About that time, Dan walks in. "Mason, you let her do what she does. She is a great cook, and you're gonna know it by the time you get well."

"But, Dan. I'm not used to this. I don't really

23

associate with a lot of people, and all these people from your church bringing this food every day is too much."

"I understand Mason. From now on, Sherry and I will be the only ones that come by. How's that?"

I didn't want to sound ungrateful, so I said, okay. Besides, the good food was better than anything I'd had in a very long time. I don't cook much since my wife died several years ago. Homemade recipes are non-existent in my house. The lemon meringue pie Sherry brought two days ago was still in my taste bud memories.

Dan and Sherry never stay too long, but long enough to talk a bit. I must admit, it has been nice having them around. They are a nice couple and I really didn't think anyone that young could be that nice. Maybe I am getting old and cynical.

Days have passed into weeks, and after two months, Dan and Sherry are still bringing me food. I can get around a lot better, but I don't want them to know just yet. Today, I met them out on the front porch. I wasn't expecting Dan to bring his lawn mower again, but he did. Sherry sat with me while her husband mowed my yard again.

"Sherry, how can I ever repay you? You and Dan have done so much for me."

"Aww Mason. It has been our pleasure to help you."

"But why? You two are young. Don't you have other things to do to keep busy?"

"Mason, we believe we are here to help others. It's part of our religion. When we do for others, we are doing it for God."

"Oh, so not for me? Just for God?"

"For God and for you, Mason. You are very dear to us now. We didn't know you before, but now we really love you as a great friend."

"Well, you're probably just gonna try to get me to go to church now. Aren't you?"

"We'd love to have you join us. But, no pressure here. We have some great people and we enjoy one another's company. The best thing about going to church, Mason, is worshipping God."

"Oh, I've never done that. I don't know if God even exists. How do you know He exists?"

"The Bible tells us all about Him. You should read the Bible, Mason. You would be surprised at what is in it."

"Oh yeah. What would surprise me?"

"Well, for starters, the Bible says God loves you. If you read in the book of John, you will find out how much. Jesus loved us so much He died on a cross for our sins."

"Yeah, yeah, yeah. I've heard all that before. I just never saw anyone who believed that stuff and lived their lives like it."

"Well Mason. I believe it."

Sherry got up and walked down the steps of the porch. She grabbed a trowel and started pulling weeds out of my flower beds. I hoped I had not offended her, but I thought about what she said. She and Dan were the perfect example of people who live out their beliefs. I was so stubborn and set in my pre-conceived ideas I had not seen it before. I felt like a heel.

Dan and Sherry finished my lawn and left to go home to do their lawn. I thanked them many times and tried to give them some money, but they would not take it. They said they'd be back tomorrow with my dinner.

That night the sleep just wouldn't come. I tossed and turned. Finally, I got up and turned on the light. I will read that book of John, I thought. What would I find that would surprise me?

"Hmm."

John says, Jesus loves me so much He went to the cross for my sins. What are sins? Am I a sinner? Sure, I've done things I am not proud of. Will that keep me from going to Heaven? Is there really a heaven and a hell?

"Wow, Jesus laid it down pretty plain for people."

I never knew Jesus was coming back to earth. I did not know Christians believe this. Not every person who says they are Christians are Christians, only the ones that live out the gospel.

"Now, I believe Dan and Sherry are truly Christians. They have lived the gospel in front of my eyes. There must be something to all of this. I have to find out for sure."

Sunday rolled around. I was sitting on my porch watching as people drove up to the little white wooden church built so long ago. There were old people, young people, children, some married, some single. Everyone seemed happy; most had big smiles on their faces. I never see people like this in town. Why are these people so happy? It must have something to do with their beliefs.

The piano is playing, and songs are being sung. It sounds inviting. I guess I could go over and sit in the back. Maybe nobody would notice me?

I hobbled over. Those words, and that melody was so catchy, I began to sing.

 *Praising the Lord! Praise the Lord!"*

Mason Volunteers

The leaves have turned brown, red, and golden in the past two weeks. The norther blew in a couple weeks ago, and the air has chilled. It has made a big difference in the landscape. I don't suppose I'll be mowing the yard much anymore until next Spring.

That is a good thing. I can use the time to do some woodworking I've put off for a while. When my wife was alive, I spent many hours in my woodworking shop making all sorts of things for our home. Since she's been gone, I have not had much desire to do anything creative.

I need another towel rack for the hall bathroom and I had planned on making it out of oak and adding a shelf on top. I need some shelf space for a few things. My wife tried to get me to make that rack and shelf several times, but I was always too busy. Now, things have changed. I have plenty of time on my hands, but she won't be here to make a fuss over my quality workmanship. I think I'll make it for her, anyway.

Now, where's the peanut butter? I'm hungry and a quick sandwich is just what I need.

"Knock. Knock. Hey Mason, are you home?"

"Come in, Sherry! What are you doing out here in the country on a Thursday?"

"Hi, Mason. Dan is across the street at the church and I decided to come over and get you to come over there and look at the choir loft."

"The choir loft? What's wrong with it?"

"Oh, remember last Sunday. Mrs. Spriggs leaned on it when she was coming down. Pastor thought he heard a noise, and he did. The bottom of the half wall has some broken spindles. Will you come over and look at it? I know you do woodworking."

"Sure, I'd be happy to look at it."

We walked over and met Dan as he was walking out the front door.

"Hi Mason. How are you?"

"Good, Dan. Sherry says you need some help with a few broken spindles on the choir loft."

"I sure do. These are the spindles I removed. You can see the wood is very old. This old church has been here a long time, and the wood is dry."

"Yes, it looks really dry, but the finish is still pretty fine."

"Yeah, I do a lot of things over here. I refinished those spindles just a few years ago myself."

"Really? You did a good job."

"Hey, that means a lot coming from a woodworker like you, Mason."

"I mean it. You did a good job. Now take me inside and let me see what it is going to take to get that loft back in shape."

We all walked inside, and I surveyed the damage. It was not that bad. I had some leftover oak wood that would work just fine, but I was going to make that towel rack. I mulled it over and decided the church needed it more than I needed
another towel rack. My wife would understand. In fact, she might be proud of me working on the church. That was something I would never have done while she was alive.

I never went to church at all until a year or so ago when I broke my ankle. Dan and Sherry took care of me, and they are the ones that helped me see I needed the Lord and the association of Christian people. The church is so friendly. It has made my widower life much more pleasant. I don't feel so alone anymore. I guess God uses people to help other people. So now, I want to help too.

"Dan, give me that tape. I want to measure how long those spindles are. I think I have enough wood in my shop to fix these in no time at all."

"Oh, Mason, that would be wonderful!" Sherry exclaimed.

"Here you go, Mason. Measure away. I'll write the numbers for you."

"Okay, good. Thanks, Dan."

It turned out I had enough wood and a little left over when the job was completed. It felt good to help Dan and Sherry, after all they had done for me.

The next Sunday, the pastor gave me credit for the repair to the choir loft and the whole congregation clapped and several of the folks thanked me personally after the service. It feels good to give back. My wife would be surprised. I was never one to do anything I didn't have to do, even for a good cause. I suppose God is changing me. Church seems to make a difference.

The leaves are falling, and the air is crisp. Sitting here on the porch with a cup of coffee, I remember back when my wife would sit here with me. We'd look at the people come and go from church every Sunday. Sometimes, she'd remark how we should check it out. I never wanted to go, and she quit asking after a time. I sure wish I had taken her. We were happy, but I think now, we might have been happier. Her cancer ate her up. I wore myself out taking care of her. We had no support group like a church to help carry our burdens. It was my fault for being so bull-headed.

Lost in my regrets, Dan and Sherry drove up. "Hey, Mason," Sherry said as she walked up on my porch. "What are you thinking about? You looked like you were in deep thought."

"Oh, it's nothing. What are you doing here?"

"Dan and I thought we'd come over and see if you

would like to go eat at Dusty's Diner for lunch."

"Yeah, Mason. It's Taco Tuesday. All you can eat!" Dan added.

"Wow, that's an offer I can't refuse. Let me get my keys."

"Just lock the door. I'm driving," Dan said.

Taco Tuesday brought many folks out. The diner was crowded, but we found a corner table. We talked to lots of the patrons; we knew most of them from church. My life is much fuller now; I am not nearly as lonely as before.

My ankle feels good. I believe it healed perfectly. Funny, how a tragic event can turn things around. I would never have met Dan and Sherry, and surely would never have started going to church if I had not broken my ankle. I guess that scripture that God turns what is meant for harm into something good is really true. It worked in my case.

We ordered and enjoyed those spicy folds of tortillas and taco meat. The salad and cheese were just enough, but the salsa was overflowing and scrumptious. Even though, my mouth was burning a little I wanted more.

"Mason, do you want some more tacos? I'm ordering two more; I'm gonna fill up!"

"Sure, give me two more. They are so good! And I love the salsa."

The waitress smiled and nodded as she walked to the

kitchen. "Coming right up!"

"Don't you just love this place?" Sherry asked. "I think we should come here every Tuesday."

"Sounds like a winning idea," I said.

Sirens caused the three of us to turn and look out the big plate-glass window. Two fire trucks were barreling down the road. One patron remarked, "I wonder where they are going?"

A couple of men got up and walked outside to see what direction the fire trucks were heading. As they walked back in, they said there was a lot of smoke to the east. "It looks like a big fire."

The waitress put our food down on the table, and we kept eating. Dan said we'd check out the fire when we finished. That sounded reasonable. We finished up in about ten minutes, paid the bill, walked to Dan's car. Another car pulled up in the parking lot. It was the pastor of the church and he was yelling, "It's the church!" He had come to the diner to pick up two of the deacons that were having lunch there. We were startled, jumped in and drove to my home. There were four fire trucks at the church when we arrived at my house. People were all around trying to help, but it was no use. The old building that was built more than a hundred years ago was in flames. The fire was so intense, a fireman came to me and told me to spray my house down with water. Dan and Sherry immediately turned on the faucet and started hosing my roof and my house with water.

We were all crying, standing in the yard, as we watched that beautiful old structure built with love so many years ago fall to the ground in a pile of ash. What great memories were gone, what opportunities to reach people for the Lord. Dan, Sherry, and I stood there as we watched the firemen remove
the bell from the steeple.

"At least, they saved the bell," the pastor said as he walked up the sidewalk of my house. "The firemen said they could do very little by the time they got here. The autumn winds fanned the flames and the old building was like dry kindling."

Sherry hugged our pastor as she wiped away tears. Dan and I put our arms around him. We knew his sorrow was even greater than ours. Slowly, the flames died, and the firemen rolled up their hoses. The burned church lay on the ground, smoldering. The smell was intense. We all four sat on my porch watching, thinking, lost in our thoughts.

Pastor asked if we could join in prayer. We bowed, and we prayed for the congregation. He said a building is just a building, but it is the people the Lord cares about. As he prayed, that realization came to me. It was the people that
made up the church, not the building.

There was peace in our hearts when the praying was done. I looked at the preacher and said, "We'll build another building. I'll help, and so will everyone else."

He smiled ear to ear. "I was hoping you'd say that, Mason. I know you were a construction engineer in your younger life. Do you think you could handle the operation?"

"Pastor, it would be my honor to do that," I said.

Sherry gave me the biggest hug. You know, I almost feel like Sherry and Dan are the children my wife and I never had. Again, it is funny how the Lord works things out when we follow Him.

New Beginnings

The little church in the country was slowly becoming a new modern facility, with a bigger sanctuary and classrooms for Bible study. Mason was having a great time planning and supervising the work.

The foundation was poured, and the rough plumbing was done. Then, the carpenters came, and they did an excellent job. They erected the framing in no time at all.

When the roofers came, it was like a whirlwind, and wiring and insulation were next on the agenda. Church members that knew about construction volunteered to do some of the work to keep the costs down. Mason was pleased to see how the members worked together and was so happy to be a part of a family. The family of God was new to him, but he was finding his place in service to the Lord. It was one of the happiest times of his life.

Months quickly passed, and every day, progress was made. The sheetrock took a while because the man appointed to do the taping and bedding got sick and couldn't do his part until later. The workers worked around the delay, and soon the walls and ceilings were ready for paint.

Sunday school teachers allowed some of the older

students to help paint their classrooms, so everyone was taking part in the construction of the new building. Friendships were strengthened and hidden talents became exposed. Some new leaders were even born. It was a fun time to be connected to a good church. Mason was counting his blessings.

Tile was laid in the foyer entrance and in both restrooms. Carpeting was put down in the sanctuary. The lighting was installed about the same time. The sound system was the last thing, and it had to be done perfectly. It had been upgraded to include sounds and lights that synchronized, and new screens on two walls were installed.

The old building could never have been remodeled like this. So, what was a tragedy turned out to be a blessing. There was a large framed picture of the old building hung in the foyer so everyone could see how the church was when it first began.

The community had watched as the new structure took shape. There was a newspaper reporter from town that visited twice and reported on the progress of the church building. An anonymous donor had given a sizable gift. It was enough to pay for new seating. Everyone tried to figure out who it was that gave, but that person remains unknown to this day.

The last thing to be done was erecting the steeple and placing the antique bell inside. It was a delicate procedure, and Daryl Hodges brought a crane from work to do it for free. Daryl and his family have been longtime members. Without a crane, putting this up would have been impossible. Daryl brought two men from his crew to help work on the church during the construction as well.

Bob, the banker, held fund raisers that brought in contributions from all over town and some even from outside the county. Members like Bob and Daryl made the difference in what the little church could do.

The church held its dedication one year after the fire. The dedication left nobody that attended with a dry eye. It was very moving. Mason was one man that grabbed a tissue several times during the service.

He had learned about God by doing God's work. He was a different man. Gone was his attitude of not needing anyone, to an attitude of gratitude for those in his life. Arrogance had disappeared and was replaced with thankfulness. Thankful that someone cared enough to reach out to him when he was in need. Today, Mason volunteers wherever he can lend a hand. He is a testament to God's patience and love. Praise the Lord!

Summer Fun

Lollipops and gumdrops,
Tennis shoes and flip-flops,
Chalk writing on the sidewalk,
Kitty cats and dogs that bark.

Colored shorts and sweaty t-shirts,
Mud pies and playing in the dirt.
Sun visors or a floppy hat,
Baseball, glove, and a bat.

Summer fun all around,
A swimming hole we have found.
Jumping in and swinging from
A hanging rope 'til we were numb.

Staying out, playing with friends,
The sun goes down, and fun ends.
Tomorrow is another day,
Of fun with friends and more play.

Summertime is the best,
No more school, only rest.

Have all the fun while you can,
Wiggle your toes in the sand.

Fall is just around the corner,
School begins again with mourners.
Children dreaming of more fun,
School has started, summer is done.

Chapter 2
Kids Have All
the Fun

KJV   Mark 10:14b
Suffer the little children to come unto me, and forbid them not: for of such is the kingdom of God.

Addie, the House Spider

There once was a big Mama spider that lived in the corner of the firewood box. The time came when she gave birth to hundreds of baby spiders. There were so many that the baby spiders were running, playing, and falling over themselves.

The lady of the house saw the activity, grabbed a broom and scraped baby spiders from the floor and the walls, and chased them in every direction they were running.

"Hurry, run this way," a baby spider yelled.

Addie saw what was happening, and she ran to the opposite corner of the firewood box and hid under a piece of log. She saw many of her brothers and sisters get swept away, but she clung to the log. After a matter of minutes, the sweeping stopped. She was safe for the moment, but knew she needed a new home.

Addie crawled to the next room, where a beautiful chandelier hung from the center of the ceiling. What a view I'd have way up there, she thought. The climb took her a while, but she eventually made it.

"This is perfect," she said. "I'll weave a web as beautiful as the crystal chandelier. Each thread will sparkle as the light hits it. My web will be big and beautiful. It will catch every visitor that is not careful. But it will not catch the eye of the lady of the house. It will be invisible in the chandelier."

Addie made her plans for a spectacular new home. She would run any other spiders off if they came near. She had claimed this place in the house for her new web. Spiders are territorial and they keep to themselves. They do not want to get caught in another's web.

Addie went to work, quickly spinning her web. She crisscrossed and then swooped the threads. Addie joined them at the ends and made large circles of the silky thread. She doubled the spin to make it strong. She wanted her web to be stronger and more intricate than her siblings' webs.

Soon, there was a pull at one end. The small web had already received a visitor. A big, ugly, black fly had flown into the corner. It was trapped. Addie slowly made her way to the fly. It saw her coming and fidgeted, trying to free itself from the web.

The web was moving back and forth, but Addie kept approaching. The movement caused the web to break and the black fly swung down into a glass prism on the chandelier. It gained its footing on the glass and soon it was freed.

It disappointed Addie that the web broke and the fly escaped. She went to work repairing the tear and strengthened it with extra threads.

"This will not happen again," she said.

Tiring from all the work, Addie fell asleep. She dreamed of a spider web with large, soft, silky threads that would never tear. The fan could blow, but the threads would never break. She would dine in pleasure every night. Her web would grow every day. Soon, it would cover the entire room. Addie had dreams and grandiose visions.

Addie was a hard worker, and before long, her web covered the chandelier. She was so proud of herself. As she admired the web one day, the lady of the house looked up.

"Oh, my, I never saw that before."

The lady of the house grabbed her dust rag and her telescopic Swiffer. She wiped down each chandelier arm and glass prism. Addie's web fell apart.

"Oh, no! Stop! Stop!"

Addie was screaming, but the lady of the house could not hear her. Addie knew she must hide, as her life was in danger. The center bulb had a dark spot on the back side. This was a great place to hide and Addie stayed hidden for the entire time the lady cleaned the chandelier.

After all the work she put in to build such a spectacular web, now it was all gone and it devastated Addie. What could she do?

44

"Should I rebuild in the same place or move to another?"

Addie thought it best to move to the bedroom. It was darker in there, and maybe she could find a quiet corner. The bedroom had angles in the ceiling and Addie considered one of those, but the ceiling fan wobbled and made too much noise. Addie thought there must be a better place in this large room.

As she surveyed the surroundings, she spotted a small table by the bed. The short legs of the table would keep a vacuum cleaner out and the underside was a perfect hiding place from humans.

"That's it!"

As she ran to the table, the lady saw her and picked her up with a paper towel. She squeezed the towel. Fortunately, Addie was in the fold and was not hurt. The lady threw the paper towel in the trash can. Addie remained still for the longest time. Then she slowly peered out of the towel. After making sure the coast was clear, she climbed out of the trash can.

Addie wanted peace and quiet. House living was too dangerous, and being an outside spider had its perks. Addie saw the patio door was open and made a run for the door. If she could just make it to the patio, surely there would be an empty corner where she could live in peace.

Passing through the doorway, suddenly it slammed

45

shut. She was caught in the metal track of the door. Would she be seen? Addie was terrified!

She convulsed as the big Labrador with a slobbery mouth came sniffing at the door. He knew Addie was there. He was trying to find her with his tongue between the glass and the metal track.

Luckily, the lady of the house thought the dog only wanted outside. She opened the door just in time for Addie to make her escape. Under the potted plant, Addie hid until the dog went away.

Finally, with everyone and everything back inside, Addie was free to explore her new area. The patio was full of fun places, like the pot of brightly colored daisies, or the fountain that had a frog on a lily pad in the center. Water splashed on Addie's legs and she shook it off.

What beauty and what wonderful homes the patio could afford, but hers would be up high away from people and the water fountain. The deepest corner of the patio had vinyl soffit trim that wrinkled. It was the perfect place to build her web. Beneath the trim, fully hidden from human view, it was ideal to trap wanderers looking for peace and quiet, too.

Addie built her wonder web within days. The silky threads looped and circled under the vinyl soffit. She still lives happily there in her new home, but don't go knocking, you may get caught in her web.

Nursing Home Visits

Children are a blessing from the Lord.
Their innocence and wonder, brings a smile,
To even the grumpiest old people,
Filled with bitterness and guile.

How can a little one do such good,
To change a wounded heart?
It's that they do not notice,
A reluctance from the start.

No, children go immediately to those in need,
Who need a warm hand, a smile, a hug.
Jump into laps and kiss old wrinkled faces,
Of people, many adults often shrug.

A trip to the nursing home,
Will open your eyes.
There are many wonderful stories,
And very few lies.

Children bring out the best in all,
Take them with you when you call.

Residents will perk up when they see,
Little children coming with you and me.

Let the little ones bring some joy,
To those confined in chairs and beds.
"Suffer the little ones to come to me."
Remember, that is what Jesus said.

Big Old Fat Lazy Cat

It was a cold, cloudy day, but the Siamese cat did not seem to care. His thick white fur kept him warm as he creeped to the edge of the garden shed. His nose was moving up and down, and I knew he smelled his prey. It was hiding in the bushes or under the garden shed. The cat was looking in each direction, trying to determine which way the smell was coming from.

He sat still at the corner and then suddenly jumped up and ran behind the wire garden fence. The prey must be on the move. It sensed the cat nearby. It was looking for a better hiding place.

I could not see as well now since the bushes hid the cat from my view except for its backside and short tail. Was it a rabbit he was stalking, or a mouse? Rabbits often live under the garden shed and appear in the Spring in my yard. Late in the autumn and in the winter, there is no sign of them, but they must be there. Hidden under the soil in their winter burrows or under bushes that camouflage their homes.

The old Siamese cat lives down the street. I've only seen him in my yard a few times. Today, he does not want to go home. He is as fat as a lazy house cat can be.

It may be hard for him to catch his prey today. Surely a little creature can outrun the big old fat lazy cat.

My garden is sleeping the cold winter away. I will till the soil in the Spring and replant my vegetables. The rabbits don't seem to bother it even though they live close by under the garden shed. There is enough food in the fence row between my yard and the field that lies behind my house. It's a paradise for small creatures.

All of a sudden, the chase was on. The big old fat lazy cat moved with precision speed, catching the prey beneath his long sharp claws. The commotion was loud as the prey screamed for its life. I pressed against the window to see.

The hawk that lives in the field behind my house was alerted and picked up its head. Hawk's eyes are sharp. He stiffened his glare and did not move.

The big old fat lazy cat grabbed the prey by its neck and trotted toward his house. I felt sorry for the little rabbit. I love watching the rabbits every spring dart from one side of my yard to the other. They eat the tall weeds and dandelions I miss.

I heard the back door of my neighbor's house slam and turned my gaze to the left. Here came Tommy with his new BB gun he got for Christmas. What was he up to? I suppose he saw the cat get the rabbit.

He was pointing the gun at the cat, or was he? The cat looked at Tommy and dropped his prey to run home.

The hawk sensed an opportunity, swooping down to catch the prey again and feast on the cat's work. As the talons of the hawk reached down to grasp the neck of the prey, Tommy's gun fired.

I looked in time to see feathers fly. The hawk immediately flew upward and away. I am sure the hawk was shocked when the bb hit the prey. Tommy's mom hollered and told Tommy to come inside. He was not allowed to shoot his gun in the backyard and especially not in my yard. He was in trouble.

I looked back at the prey. It lay on the ground, motionless. The cat was gone. The hawk was gone. Tommy was inside and the prey lay still in my yard. I was sad to think a little rabbit died that day and would not be scurrying across my lawn this spring.

I decided to get a shovel from the garage and go bury it behind my garden. As I approached, I burst out laughing. The prey was not a rabbit at all. It was a big old fat rat! I was so glad it was gone. Something had chewed on my okra plants last summer, and now I knew what it was. Now, I won't have that problem this year.

Then, as I touched it with my shovel, the rat came alive! It had only been stunned by the bb. It ran off in the opposite direction. I guess my okra plants will suffer again this year.

Imaginations of a Garment Thief

"Why is the imagination so important?" I asked Mrs. Williford. She was my third-grade teacher, and about the smartest woman I ever met.

Mrs. Williford quickly replied, "You can be anything you want to be, if you can imagine it."

She said I had promise. She let me sit at her desk when she had to go to the office for copies or whatever. Mrs. Williford would tell the class I was in charge. I imagined being a teacher someday.

She was an unusual teacher; she actually took an interest in her students. She knew my parents were poor, and my opportunities were somewhat limited. But she also encouraged me. I was timid, and she tried to help me overcome that shyness. That was before I learned who I was, a child of God, equipped with power from on high.

I suppose several of the teachers in my school, and especially my principal, helped us students learn about

God. My folks didn't go to church, so school was the only place I was going to hear about Him. Unless you count the many times my parents yelled his name in anger. Why, I didn't know God had so many names!

My brother and I stayed out of the way when Mom and Dad were calling on the Lord. Most times, we hit that screen door a runnin'. It would fly open and we'd jump off the porch and head for the pasture. The pasture was out back behind our house. It was just open land with a few scraggly mesquite trees, some rocks, and a few cows. Those cows stayed at the back where the only grass grew. That pasture was so big we rarely saw any animals.

The big open spot was a dried-up lakebed. It was a long time ago when there was water in it. It was dry and cracked hardpan clay soil now. Nothing would grow in it. When the rains came, that soil was like quicksand. If you got stuck in it, you'd better come out of your shoes and leave them there.

When it dried up, you could get the shoes back, but they might never be the same. That soil was a killer. If a cow ever walked into it while it was wet, it got stuck. So, we did not go to the pasture during the rainy spells.

Our friends, Bob and Darla, also brother and sister, lived down the road and played with us in the pasture quite often. There were many large rocks that surrounded that open spot. Rocks were big enough for us to sit on and hide behind. Two of the rocks were elongated and lay side by side. There was actually a little cave between these two rocks because the dirt had washed out years ago. This was a good place to hide while we played hide and seek.

We played cowboys and Indians, played pioneers on the frontier, played all sorts of games around those rocks. We built forts and imagined all kinds of things.

My favorite imaginations were of dinosaurs. I would sit on top of one of those rocks and blast out a dinosaur roar that permeated the whole valley and the hill next to it. My friends would come running, making roaring sounds too. I could roar louder than all of them. They were not as intrigued by the theropods and sauropods as I was.

I could imagine the big thunderous steps of a creature coming through the pasture. Dinosaurs would roar and scream, calling for prey. Hoping to scare the smaller creatures to run and show themselves. The giant monsters would devour them. Tyrannosaurus Rex was walking this way.

"Stop, listen!" I would say to Darla. "Can you hear it?"

"No," she would say, with eyes bulging.

I'd whisper, "Come on, let's hide before it gets here."

With hearts pounding and hard breathing, we'd hide between the rocks and wait.

In a little while, the boys would come looking for us. They would yell our names. We would stay still and pray the dinosaurs didn't get them. When they tired of looking for us, we'd jump out from our hiding place and laugh.

Sometimes, we would walk to the creek and fish for crawdads. It was easy to catch crawdads if the creek had muddy water in it. Tie a string to a stick and put some bacon on it. Crawdads love bacon. We didn't eat them like other people do, but we took the big ones and had races with them. What fun times we had.

Bob and Darla had a teenage sister, Ginger. She must have thought she was the prettiest thing around, the way she flitted in front of her boyfriends. Fancy clothes and lots of make-up set those boys up for defeat. We made fun of her behind her back when we sprayed her cologne in the air like air freshener. She didn't like us hanging around, and was always telling us to get lost.

She had some nice clothes. She always wore a lot of can-cans (petticoats) with those fancy skirts. One day, the devil got hold of us. Darla and I took some of her skirts, blouses, and petticoats from the clothesline. We took them to the pasture. We would bring them back later that day, of course.

We imagined being actresses, so Darla and I dressed up. We changed our outfits several times because we had about a dozen skirts, blouses and petticoats that belonged to Ginger. We had so much fun that day.

Those elongated rocks that sat on the side of the hill by the dried-up lakebed made a perfect dressing room. The space between the rocks had been washed out years before and made a little cave tall enough for us to stand in. Completely hidden by the rocks on both sides, it was a hiding place, a cabin, or a dressing room. That little cave became whatever game our imaginations wanted to play. That day we were performing plays, and the boys were our audience. We got standing ovations.

Our Mom never bothered us when we were playing out in the pasture. We could be out there all day long. This day she decided she was going to town and wanted my brother and me to go with her.

Bob and Darla had to go home. We decided we could leave Ginger's clothes in the little cave between the rocks. Then, the next day, we could come back and play some more. After that, Darla could take them home and Ginger would never know we used them. Little did we know, a thunderstorm was coming in that night.

How could we have known it was going to rain for 3 days straight? We couldn't leave the house. I was worried, and so was my brother. I could just imagine what Bob and Darla were going through. I hoped Ginger had enough clothes without the ones hidden in the cave. Maybe she would not miss them at all.

It finally stopped raining. My brother and I went to

the edge of the pasture. It was muddy, and that mud was sticky. I took a few steps and began to sink. I went to another area and tried there; same thing.

"We've gotta get those clothes!" my brother said.

"I know, I know. But how?"

He took a few steps and sunk up to his ankles.

"Now, look what you've done!" I screamed at him. "You better get that mud off those good shoes. Mom, will skin you alive!"

It was a week later before we could get to those rocks at the big clear spot. Darla and Bob came with my brother and me to retrieve them. The skirts had been brightly colored and ruffled, but the can-cans were white and pastel colors. The netting they were made from was light-weight, and you might say 'fine threaded'.

We all peered into the space between the rocks. How could we have known those rocks were on an incline? How could we have known the rain would cause a mud slide right between those rocks?

"Oh, no! Look at that!" I gasped.

Darla replied, "They're gone!"

The boys said, "Move over, let us see!"

To our amazement, not only were the clothes gone, but the little cave was filled in and was no longer there. The mudslide buried the clothes and filled in the space between the rocks. It would never be the same.

All the clothes were gone. We started to dig a little in

that still soft mud. I found the edge of a can-can but when I pulled it; it ripped in a million pieces. Each of us tried to retrieve some garments, but not one came out whole. The material had deteriorated, and it fell apart in our hands.

What could we do? We decided those garments were to be buried forever. No one would mention this to anyone. It was a secret between the four of us. We shook hands on it.

Bob and Darla were pacing with worry, scared their big sister would find out. They said she'd been looking for some of those clothes, and they had played ignorant of the whole thing.

Their stepmom was the one we were most afraid of, but she had no idea what happened to those clothes, either. Bob and Darla were forced to help as every closet and drawer in the entire house was searched. Their stepmom suspected Ginger had given them away to a friend. Ginger was in trouble for a while. Their stepmom never suspected the younger kids. That was good for all of us!

I guess imagination can get you into trouble sometimes, but it sure was fun being an actress on the stage, or a dinosaur, or a teacher. With imagination, you can be anything, just like Mrs. Williford said.

It was many years later when one day I saw Ginger and her stepmom in a clothing store. We talked for a while, and I remembered what we had done with Ginger's clothes. I told them about it and asked for forgiveness. They both laughed, and said it was okay. I knew I had done wrong and needed to make amends. I bought the garments Ginger was trying on that day as a way to make up for the ones we had taken. It is never too late to make things right.

Tiger Changed His Mind

"Mom, Tiger did not come eat his food last night."

"Oh, honey. We can't count on him coming every night. Tiger is a feral cat, and he roams around the entire neighborhood. He probably ate somewhere else last night."

"But he usually comes and eats here."

"Yes, he usually does, but not every night. Now, it's time for you to eat your breakfast."

Mom put the cereal on the table and opened the refrigerator to get the milk as little Cassie put her bowl on the table.

"You love that pink cereal bowl, don't you?" Mom said.

"Yes, it's my favorite."

"I remember when you and Nana painted it, and fired it in the kiln."

"Mom, when are we going to see Nana again?"

"Maybe next week. I'll be off on Monday and we can go spend the whole weekend. Would you like that, Cassie?"

"Very much. I want to see Nana. We can make some more bowls. We can make one for Tiger. Then, he would be sure and come to eat his dinner."

*****

Tiger roamed the neighborhood looking for food and looking for warm places to nap. His favorite place was under the brown and green storage building in Mr. Gates' backyard. There was a big dugout space at the back of the building and the space underneath was large enough to stretch out, but small enough to be cozy. Tiger claimed it for his own. However, there were times he was forced to fight for it with other cats and an occasional opossum.

Tiger got his name fair and square. He was a fighter and had the scars to prove it. The nip out of the corner of his ear was a badge of honor. Tiger never ran from a fight with another animal.

Tiger could run fast, though, and he showed it whenever Cassie saw him on the porch and tried to pet him. Tiger was not having any little girl catch him, or pet him. He was wild and he liked being wild.

"No human will ever tame me," he said. "No cat food is worth being captured by humans."

*****

"Mom, he is here!"

"Don't scare him, Cassie."

"I won't. I just want to watch him eat."

"Ok, but don't open the door. You will scare him."

"I know, Mom, but how will I ever pet him?"

"He is wild, Cassie. He would not make a good pet."

"But, Mom."

"No, Cassie. If you want a cat, we will get one from the shelter that is already tame. You don't need a wild cat."

Cassie was sad and walked away from the door. Tiger looked up from his meal. Cassie was no longer standing there watching him. He had heard what Mom said to Cassie.

"How dare her say I am wild and would not make a good pet," Tiger said under his breath.

He was so surprised by Mom's statements he was no longer hungry. He walked away slowly, wishing Cassie would open the door so he could act surprised and run away like he always did. Today, the door did not open.

Tiger was disappointed and went to Mr. Gates' shed for a nap. He would come back later for another meal. Surely, he would see Cassie then.

The day lingered on, and later in the afternoon, Tiger met another neighborhood cat along Pine Street as he strolled back over to Cassie's.

"Hey, Fluffball. How's life treating you?" Tiger puffed out his chest as he swiped his tail back and forth.

"Life is good. I got my nails done today," she said as she swished her tail in his direction.

"Nails, heh? I've got sharp claws, not prissy nails," he gruffed back.

"Mine are sharp too, but manicured," she said as she raised her head high and walked in the opposite direction.

"Ah! Who needs an owner? I've got my freedom!" Tiger growled.

"And I've got a soft bed waiting for me at home."

Tiger had heard enough and crossed the street and went behind the bushes, heading to the backyard of Cassie's home.

When he got there, a pink bowl with Cassie's name on it sat on the porch step. There was sweetened milk in the bowl. It tasted pretty good and the milk made Tiger sleepy. He decided to ball up on the soft cushion that sat on the porch rocker. The sun was shining, and it was warm, the perfect place and time for a nap.

As Tiger dreamed dreams of catching mice and birds, Cassie saw him asleep in the chair. She quietly opened the door and placed both hands quickly around Tiger's chest. She had him in her grasp.

Tiger awoke in horror. He was caught. His first thought was to fight. He could extend his claws and scratch Cassie and get away. Then, the thought of being a pet appealed to him more, and he relaxed in her arms. She held him close to her body, and Tiger could feel her heartbeat. She rubbed his head with her hand, and it felt so good. He wanted more and more petting.

"Oh, yes," he said to himself. "More, more, on the other side. Yeah, that's it."

Tiger was caught, and he was loving it. Cassie took him inside the house and it smelled so good. Mom was cooking something delightful. Cassie took Tiger to the couch and placed him on a big cushy pillow and petted him more, rubbing the underside of his neck.

"Tiger, I love you," Cassie said.

Mom said, "Cassie, he may not want to be an inside cat. He has had his freedom outside."

"I'll take him outside sometimes, but he seems to like it in here."

Tiger stood on the pillow and kneaded it with his feet. He was purring loudly. Cassie continued to pet Tiger for the rest of the day. He slept at the end of her bed that night. Tiger never missed the outdoors again. He loved being known as Cassie's cat.

No Jogging in the Snow

As the snow departs from this land,
I stand and shout with clapping hands.
I hate the cold, cold winter days,
I have things to do instead of gaze
Through frozen window panes.

Warmer temps are what I long for,
Bright, sunny days I want more.
Walking without coats, gloves, and scarves,
Summer for me, no winter garb,
Judy won't agree, neither will Barb.

Exercise is walking slow,
On dry pavement with no snow.
Jogging clothes and tennies on my feet,
Boots will cut it with ice and sleet,
Days like that, I pass and sleep.

The girls say, "Come on, get out of bed,"
I say, "No, I'm just a sleepy head.
Wake me when winter is all gone,
I'll be ready to go before the dawn."
Spring is near, but Summer is what I long.

Chapter 3
A Woman's Voice

The Birthday Dinner

My son will be here in about 30 minutes, I said to myself as the words slipped from my mouth. I was running behind. Working the last contract took longer than I expected, and then the grocery shopping time was extended because of the long lines in the checkout.

I don't know why I think I have to have it all done by the time he arrives. He has watched me cook his whole life, but his birthday dinner is special. I want to have time to sit and chat for a while. I rarely get to see him these days. We are both working such long hours, and he lives a good drive from me. Birthdays and holidays are about the only time we get together and have a chance to talk one on one.

I wonder who he is dating now? His last girlfriend left him in a bad way. He said he would not be anxious to get involved again until some time has passed. Our last phone conversation gave me the impression he had found someone, but was not ready to share the news. Maybe today he will.

I am making his requested meal with meatloaf, mashed potatoes, pea salad, and his favorite German chocolate cake is already iced and waiting for the birthday candles. Yes, I am going to put candles on it, even if he says it is not necessary. I like making a fuss over my only son. His dad has been gone for a long time now, and we are the only ones left on this side of the family.

So, I pull out my largest mixing bowl and put the ground beef in with some salt and pepper. I add a couple of eggs and mix well. Eggs help it bind together. Now, I add my secret ingredient, the tomato sauce. It makes my meatloaf nice and moist. I mix it well.

Chopping onions and celery comes next. Add it in, and I sprinkle some garlic powder. I use garlic in everything; it is a healthful ingredient. About that time, the doorbell rings. He is here!

I rush to the door and say, "Come in!"

"Hi, Mom!" he says as he hugs me and pecks me on the cheek.

"Come into the kitchen. I got home late and I'm still putting the meatloaf together."

"Oh, that's good. I've got a favor to ask."

"What's that?"

"Can we add some extra ingredients to the meatloaf?"

"My meatloaf? Well, sure. What did you have in mind?"

"Recently I had some Mexican meatloaf, and I liked

it."

"Mexican meatloaf? Never heard of it, but if you like it, we will try it."

"Good. We just need to add some seeded jalapeno peppers and some cumin."

"Do you have some?"

"Oh yes, you should know I always have those items."

We both laughed. I love Mexican food and make it quite often. So having cumin, chili powder, and peppers in my pantry is always a sure thing. Fresh jalapenos and cilantro in the fridge are a 50/50 chance. Today, he is lucky I just came from the store. The fridge is fully stocked and those shiny green jalapenos are all his.

"Grab the peppers from the fridge and you can wash them and take out the seeds. Dice them for me too, please."

"Sure thing, Mom. I love helping you in the kitchen, just like old times."

I smiled. My heart was full. Working on the meatloaf brought back some good memories of when he was younger. I am a very blessed woman. My son is spending his birthday with me instead of being out at some party with his friends. I know how special this day is to him, but to me, it is even more special. A mom remembers the birth of her child on his birthday with memories the child has only heard about. Her experiences and memories are hers alone.

I put about a third of a can of diced carrots into the meat mixture as my son prepared the peppers. We added some hot spices and then it was time to crumble the club crackers. When the mixture was the right texture, we put it in the oven for an hour and a half.

We made the potatoes and salad as the meatloaf cooked. The table was set since last night. I have been looking forward to this dinner for a few days. I have a present for my son, but he has not spotted it yet. It is sitting on the coffee table in the living room. He has been too busy with me in the kitchen to notice.

I think I will save it until the dinner is finished. He will want to spend a lot of time looking at it when he realizes this laptop computer is his birthday gift. I am excited to give him this, as his old one is on its last leg. There will be no shirts or after shave this year, but something he really needs and wants.

"Boy, that meatloaf is smelling so good!"

"Yes, it is," I reply. "We're finished in here for a while. Let's get a drink and go sit on the back patio."

"I was just about to say the same thing."

He poured us each a glass of iced tea and we went outside. The day was over and the sun was setting in the west.

"Look, what a beautiful sunset," I said.

We admired the sky and talked about a variety of

subjects. It was the special time I needed with my son. Memories like these last a lifetime.

The aroma of the meatloaf reached us just in time to remove it from the oven. It had a nice crust on top from the bacon strips and ketchup we put on it midway during the cooking.

Our dinner was everything I planned it to be. Just the two of us instead of a group. We both needed this special time. We can always invite friends and neighbors, but tonight we needed individual time to talk about important things. My son needed this time with me as much as I needed it with him.

I lit the candles, and he made a wish and blew them out. He would not tell me his wish, but I bet I know what it was.

When I gave him his gift, he was very surprised and happy. He said he had to set it up immediately. We took it to the kitchen table, and he fiddled with it as I cleaned up the dishes. I knew he would love it and his head would be in that computer all night after I gave it to him. I am glad I waited.

"Mom, this computer is awesome. It is everything I wanted in a computer and I'll have it going in no time at all. What's your wi-Fi?"

I gave him the code and went back to my dishes.

After about thirty minutes, I was getting fidgety. I wanted to spend more time with him, but he said it would only take a couple more minutes and then, he had something he wanted to show me.

It was a group of photos of him and his new girlfriend, Erica. He said he was saving the best news for last. He is in a serious relationship and will be bringing her by to meet me next week. We spent the next three hours talking about how they met, what they have done, and what their plans are for the future. I don't think we will have another birthday dinner with just the two of us. My family is growing again, and I am happy because he is happy.

Love Is...

Love, what is love? He said he loves me, but how do I know he even knows what the word means? He kissed me, held me tight, looked me in the eye, and whispered those three words over and over again. So many words I did not hear, because my mind went all blurry when he said those three most important words.

"I love you," I said back. Was I in my right mind? Do I really love him like he wants me to? I don't know yet. I have strong feelings for him, but are those feelings enough to make a lifelong commitment to a man I have only known for a short while?

I wish I had someone to talk to about this situation. My grandmother told me many years ago that she and my granddad only knew one another for a few weeks before they got married. After 41 years of marriage, he passed away. She said she never regretted marrying him, but how did she know for certain she was making the right choice?

She said she made a commitment, and that was the choice. You learn to love more and more the longer you are together. Was it easier back then, when people made commitments and refused to break a commitment because things did not go the way they expected? I think it was. What was expected of a couple was different back then, and there were not so many options as today.

Life was simpler then, because the roles were more clearly defined. Expectations were known on a general level and society was more centered. Options don't necessarily make things better, but often options make things harder.

Love. Love is a word that is too easily used and rarely used in full commitment. That is why it scared me, when he told me of his love. He wants me to be his wife, but I was engaged before. My ex-fiance did me wrong, so how will I know it won't happen to me again like before? I might not recover the second time. This is a big decision, and he caught me off guard. I was not expecting him to ask me to marry him this soon. His love seems real and everything looks good on the surface, but how can I know?

How did my grandmother know back then? Was she afraid as I am afraid? She took the chance and my granddad was an awesome dad, according to my mom, and I assume an awesome husband. Will my guy be like him? He would have big shoes to fill if he was even the least bit like my granddad. Should I compare him? Is that fair? He is not the same, and these are different times.

How are we to measure one's character? Has he

always told me the truth? Have his friends told me the truth, and what about his past? Does it show who he really is, and do I know it all? I have questions and until I know the answers, my answer to his question must be, "It is too soon."

I want to love him and be loved by him. I want to be married. More time is needed for me to know him better, and his family. Grandmother always said, "You marry the family as well as the man."

That was good advice. I wish I had listened to her the first time. Things would be different now if I had only listened to her when she was here.

She has been gone a long time now, but it seems like only yesterday we sat on her front porch and discussed life. I miss her so. Grandmother was a good listener, and her sweet tea was the best. If only we could sit there again. She would tell me things I need to hear, even if I do not want to hear them.

My grandmother had great intuition, and I wish she could meet this handsome, gentle man that says he loves me. She was a good judge of character, and she never minced her words, even though they were said in love.

She knew love was the greatest gift the world has ever known. Love has many forms, and the love between two people in a romantic fashion is greatly sought after. Love between parents, grandparents, and children is strong; and friendship love is worthy of admiration. Grandmother told me the greatest love is God's love for his people. It outweighs all the others.

So, I will spend some time with God, and ask Him to show me what to do about my decision to love this man and give my life to him. God loves me more, but I want the man I marry to love me as much as he can. If God gives him the capacity to love me even more, I want that kind of love.

We will make our decision to love and commit to each other in front of God and witnesses. It will be a real understanding of what we are doing, not just going through the motions of an expected ceremony. We will not just memorize some words, but we will say them with understanding in our hearts and mean them from the bottom of our souls.

Marriage is not to be entered into lightly, as the preacher will say. We will be somber and yet joyful in making this statement to one another in front of the whole world. When our heads are clear and our hearts are on fire, we will take the steps to a new life shared by two people.

I have time to make the right decision. I have time to make up my mind and when I do, there will be no delaying. We will start living the life we were made for, sharing our time, our resources, our efforts, our love.

My heart is happy when I think of him. I feel like dancing, twirling, moving to the rhythm of my soul. I hear music whispering in the wind as the leaves ripple on their branches. Nothing can keep me from the joy that is bursting from within. I have never felt this kind of love before, and it is immersing me from top to bottom. Nobody knows what I am feeling. It is a secret that wants to escape from my mouth and spread like pollen blown by the breeze. How can I contain it? **Love is so grand! Love is so grand!! Love is so grand!!!**

I'm Not Lucy Goosey

No matter what people say, I am not Lucy Goosey. I know I look a lot like her, but I am in no way like her in my actions. Why, I hear tell, she had her babies in someone else's nest. I would never do something like that.

People say she is often seen in public places with a public face. Do you know what I mean? Yes, Lucy Goosey is a woman of which I do not associate.

It is true, my name is Lucy. And it is true, I am a goose. A very proud greylag goose at that! I do all the goosey things other geese do, but I am unique. I have a brain that is bigger than all my peers, and I can see the world in a different way from my friends. They only seem interested in the occasional seed on the ground or bug flying around their heads.

Let me tell you, there is a lot more going on in the goose world than this. Sure, some of my own family members have no clue about higher things. I try to share important revelations with them, but most times, I am just brushed off like lint on your trousers.

Having a bigger brain that can think differently can have its obstacles. Sometimes, I just don't fit into the circles I think I should. All the honking that goes on can be irritating to a bird that is a deep thinker. They chase one another all over the yard, honking like it is something special. It is most irritating.

I find peace down by the pond. There is a small peninsula that juts out into the water on the southern side. The willow tree that grows there is most welcoming. I find a wet, muddy patch of ground under the tree and sit there and watch the clouds roll by. My friends wonder what I am doing. I am just sitting there thinking about how I can make life better for my gaggle of geese.

My gaggle seems happy enough if they are well fed, but there is more to life than filling your belly. Old Mother Goose, that's what we call Mrs. Smith. The farmer's wife knows there is more to life. I've seen her come down to the pond many times and stand there talking out loud, and sometimes crying. I am not sure who she is talking to, but somebody is listening because when she finishes, she is smiling and shaking her head ok.

I think I have the same kind of intelligence as Mrs. Smith. I know I stand up higher than other geese. My cousin said I just have a longer neck, but what does he know?

There is a lot more to being an exceptional goose or gander than just flying in a V wedge. Anyone can do that. That is why we take turns. However, Gomer sure messed up the last time we went to Canada. That was the messiest pointing I've ever seen. He would head out in one direction and in no time at all, we were flying in the opposite direction. It added many miles to our trip. I think that gander got hit on the head the last time he fell from the sky.

"Goofy would be a better name for Gomer."

I kept telling the gaggle we should just skip Gomer, but they like to give him his turn.

"Go figure! That's why I know I have superior intelligence. Who would let the dumbest lead?"

It looks like everyone is heading for the cornfield. There is a lot of corn left on the ground after harvest. I think I'll mosey on over there myself. These pretty pink legs of mine need a nice walk. Why spend half a day looking for a meal, when all that corn is just begging to be eaten?

"Oh, no! Can it be? Are my eyes just deceiving me?"

"Hey there, Lucy Goosey!" Jimmy the Grackle hollers.

"What are you doing here?" I ask.

"Chowing down, just like you, sweetie pie!" He moves over closer to me, eyeing my mouth.

"You leave my orange bill alone, Jimmy Grackle!"

The last time I saw this fowl, he kept trying to peck my orange bill. I think he was drunk on that grain from the silo that spilled. He was always a nuisance.

"Jimmy Grackle, you go to the other side of the field and leave me alone!"

"Don't get your feathers ruffled. I'm leaving."

That was too close for comfort. Old grackles can ruin a good meal.

"Mmm, this is quite good corn." I peck away.

When it is time for a nap, I make my way back to the willow tree by the pond. The grass that grows by the edge of the water makes a perfect dessert. I like to save that for last. It leaves a sweet taste in my mouth.

Aww, the beauty of the pond, I marvel. I love being alone. With the noise of the gaggle in the far distance, I can concentrate on more important things, like clouds floating by at a slow rate of speed, not nearly as fast as we can fly. Naptime is good.

I awake at the sound of a human. Mrs. Smith is back. She is angry; she is yelling at someone, but I see nobody there. I wonder who is she talking to? She falls down on her knees. Now, she is pounding the dirt with her fists. She seems very upset.

I want to go over and comfort her, but she doesn't seem to be ready for that. She is still talking loudly. Now, her tears are flowing like rain. She is snorting and blowing her nose. It's kinda nasty. I wonder what should

I do?

Mrs. Smith lies down on the dirt. I've never seen her do that before. She usually does not like mud, but maybe she is more like me than I thought. This mud feels good. I snuggle down a little deeper.

She's quiet now. She is still sniffling and crying a bit. Maybe I'll wander over a little closer.

She sees me coming closer and now she is slowly raising her body up on her elbows. She is looking right at me. I stop. I look at her and then I look away. Looking up at the clouds, and then lowering my eyes, I peer into hers again. She sighs.

I look up again and I can see from the corner of my eye she is now looking up, too. There is a big gray cloud coming by now, it has a funny shape. It is very interesting as the shades of gray are moving around quickly from one side to the other. It is gray like me, so it must be a good cloud.

Mrs. Smith raises up a bit more, and is now sitting on the ground. She is holding out her hand to me and moving her fingers. I wonder what she is thinking. Does she want me to come over near her?

I am a little shy around humans, but maybe it's okay to befriend her. Oh yes, she is pulling out a carrot from her apron; a carrot with the top attached. I love carrot tops. Sure enough, she is eating the carrot.

"Hey, give me the carrot top!" I am screaming inside

my mind.

Yeah, I waddle over there and she tosses the top to me. I knew what she was thinking! It's proof, I am more intelligent than my peers.

Mrs. Smith reaches out to touch my back. I don't know why she is rubbing my back, but it feels good.

"Oh yeah, just behind my neck, and all the way down my back. Ohhhh. That's good. I like it."

Mrs. Smith is smiling now. She is saying something and I think she is talking to me. She is looking right into my eyes. Yes, she is trying to communicate. How awesome!

"I'm not sure she is understanding me, but I sure like her petting. We'll do this again, but now I need to get back to the gaggle before all the corn is gone."

Author to Author

If I had a dream
I'd dream of you.
If I had a dollar
I wouldn't be blue.

If you had a dime
It would be sublime.

Me and you,
And you and me
I promise that's how,
It would be.

That's never here,
That's never there.
All we've got
Is thin air.

Broke and broker,
That's who we are.
Up and down,
Never getting very far.

One day things will change,
On every word they will hang.
You'll know it's not all show,
We'll be rolling in the dough.

Fame and fortune one day soon,
Hope doesn't burst like a balloon.
No, it can't 'cause words endure,
Guaranteed, our books allure.

Birthday Interrupted

The sun was going down as I crossed the Mackinac Bridge going south. I wanted to get home before dark, but I didn't know if I could make it or not. Would my parents be waiting in the driveway? I hoped not. It was so cold out. I didn't want them to have to wait for me to get there.

My trip to the U.P., the Upper Peninsula, was more than I had bargained for. Meeting that publisher in Sault St. Marie was a bad idea. Sure, I want readers from Canada, but not that bad. What a jerk he was! How dare he say to me the things he did? He must have thought I was stupid, so glad I went by myself. My husband would have punched him in the face.

Thinking of my husband, maybe he got off early from work. Maybe he is home already. That would be great if he was there when my parents arrive. If only my cell phone hadn't fallen out of my purse, and if only that car had not run over it just as I spotted it on the ground. What a day, what a birthday this is going to be!

I am just so glad I have everything ready for our

dinner tonight. Spiral sliced ham with that roast pepper chutney is going to be so delicious. I'll slow down my mind when I get home. We will have a lovely dinner and then, birthday cake. Everyone will sing 'Happy Birthday' to me, and mom will shed a tear like she always does.

Oh, I forgot to call Carol to tell her to bring those flavored coffees my mom loves. Maybe she will think about it before she drives over. Carol and Dave are always late. I won't be able to have them go back and get them. Maybe I should just stop at the grocery store and get some. I'll be driving right by a quick stop store. Yeah, I could do a quick stop. I am going to need to get around this slow poke tractor trailer though.

C'mon man! I'm in a hurry! I've got miles to make before I hit Gaylord. Some people think they are the only ones on the road. C'mon, move over!

"Ok, it's about time. See 'ya, buddy!"

The lines on the highway are blurred. It's a little icy on the edges. No problem, I have snow tires. 70, 75, 80, oh, ok 85, here we go!

"No! Deer! I-I-I-I-I-I-I."

The sound of the crashing vehicle, the flashing lights, the warm sweet taste in my mouth only lasted a few seconds, I think.

There were bright lights in my eyes the next time I was aware of anything. I could hear people talking, like whispering. I didn't know who it was or what they were saying. Then something very cold touched my torso. It was freezing. I was on my back, but I could not raise up my head. Nothing would move. Was I paralyzed? "Where am I?" I kept saying.

No one would answer me. I could see no faces. I was not scared, but I needed some answers. Nothing was hurting, so I must be paralyzed. Then, the fear came over me. I passed out.

It was the next day when I awoke again. My husband and my parents were there in the hospital room with me. I had some broken ribs, a concussion and a few cuts and bruises. My lip had a gash on one side where I bit myself during the crash. My car was totaled, my husband informed me, but I was going to be alright.

I will live for another birthday my mom happily told me. I was so glad to see them all, and their hugs meant more than ever before. How could I have let myself get in such a rush that I would put myself in danger like that?

That was so stupid, to get aggravated with someone driving slower and safer. I needed to slow down. My husband told me the tractor trailer driver called the police and then came to the hospital and stayed until my family arrived.

"Is he still here?" I asked.

"No, he had to get going. He had a tight schedule, but

he left this bouquet of flowers for you, and said he would pray for you to get well quickly."

Tears welled up in my eyes, and I knew how blessed I was. My birthday gift was the chance to have another birthday.

Crazy Mary

When we were kids, my brother and I would walk to the city park. The swings were iron frames with metal chains and wooden seats. The high slide for older kids had a hump in the center, making it lots more fun. That slide was shiny metal, and it got hot in the summer sun. During the hottest part of the day, the sun shone directly on it and nobody could use it. But in the late afternoon, the sun moved. It was in the shade.

We used to take wax paper and rub it all over that slide. It would make it easier to slide down and we could go faster. We loved the slide and the swings, but we also loved a flat disk painted like a pie with each slice a different color. There were bars in between each pie slice and we would sit on a colored slice and one person would push the disk around and around. You had to hold on tight; that disk could swing you right off. Landing in the dirt hurt. Getting hit in the head from its spinning hurt more. Many kids were injured on that contraption.

We were tough in those days. We got hurt, wiped off the blood, spit on the scrape, and kept playing. We grew up tough, or we didn't make it. Our parents did not baby us. They got mad if we got hurt, so we kept it to ourselves.

Sometimes, when we went to the park, we would see a girl there named Mary. She did not live very far away. We would talk to her sometimes and swing on the swings with her. She never talked much because she talked funny. She was hard to understand, and sometimes her words did not make sense.

Mary was not pretty; she had a strange look about her. We recognized as kids she was different. We tried to play with her, but she had trouble following the rules of games. She often stood alone and to the side. Mary was mentally retarded and could not understand many things.

One day, four young boys were making fun of her and calling her names. I heard them say, "Crazy Mary!" That's what they often called her. She did not cry, but she stood there, unable to speak back. My brother and I ran those boys off. We told them to leave her alone. We played with Mary for the rest of the day.

Mary's mother was single, and they were very poor. Mary went to school in clothing that was not very desirable. I often saw Mary with a dirty face and dirty hair. Her body did not smell good, and most people stayed far away from her.

I never knew what happened to Mary because she started going to a different school, and we stopped going to the park. After that time in our lives, there were days we were driving in town and my brother and I would spot her walking home. The only times we saw her was when she was walking.

Fifty years have come and gone and I have rarely thought about Mary. I never wondered what happened to her, what kind of life she had. I never thought about reaching out to her, trying to help her. It just never dawned on me that was my job to do. Maybe it wasn't. But how often do we overlook those around us that are different and ignore them? They might not be as smart as us, as rich as us, as good looking. There are many reasons we choose to overlook more unfortunate people.

Being kind means more than smiling and walking away. Sometimes, it means reaching out and making someone's life better.

I read an obituary recently that brought back memories of Mary. There was her photo in the newspaper. She was much older, but she still had that funny look. It was her. I had never known her last name. I never knew exactly where she lived. The obituary stated the facts about her life. I read it, eager to know more. Her mother had been disabled when Mary was a young child. She was unable to walk, and Mary took care of her mother instead of her mother taking care of her.

There were case workers that looked in on her, but they had very few relatives, and very little help. There were not as many social programs in those days. Mary graduated from high school, though it was a special program for those that are learning disabled.

She found a job at a factory on an assembly line. She walked to work on the other side of town every day. Mary loved her job and felt proud of it. She only missed work if she was very sick. She was fairly healthy, because she got lots of exercise walking every day.

With a regular paycheck, she and her mother lived better than they had during Mary's younger life. She had very few friends, but she was used to being alone. When her mother died, Mary felt the loneliness more than she ever had before. She continued to work at her job, but her enthusiasm had diminished.

Her obituary said there would only be a graveside service, no funeral. I decided I would go, and give Mary some of my time that I was too busy to give before. It was a nice day, the sun was shining, a light breeze was blowing. The canopy at the gravesite flapped in the breeze, making a rhythmic sound. I swear there were angels there, and to my surprise, there was not an empty seat. People stood all around the tent, saying their goodbyes to Mary.

She was a quiet soul, had little in life, but somehow touched many people's lives. I wondered how many people there felt like I did. I did not do enough to make Mary's life better. How many were there out of guilt? How many were there because they loved her and would miss her? How many were indebted to her for her kindness to them?

I guess I'll never know this side of heaven. When I get there though, I know Mary will be there. She will not talk funny anymore. She will have a bright shiny robe, and she will be beautiful. Mary, I want to be more like you.

A Good Name

It was a chilly December morning, and I was at a real estate conference in a city far away from home. There were prepared speeches and a long list of speakers to choose from on the agenda. I studied the list and decided which ones I would most benefit from as I planned my day.

The hotel breakfast was okay, but nothing to rave about. The coffee was good, though. I had my usual two cups and put away my dishes. I looked down the list and found the room number of the first speaker, and took the elevator to the next floor. This hotel was humongous and people were crowded in every room I walked past.

The lettering on the doors was hard to read and confusing. People were standing in the way and finding a room number became a chore. Talking and noise were taking its toll on my senses. Beginning to feel uneasy, like coming here was not a good idea, crossed my mind several times.

Then the hall widened, and the crowd eased. The maroon carpet with gold swirls seemed to lead me to an open door. There was no one standing at the door, so I slipped in without anyone noticing. I was unsure where I was, but the speaker had a pleasant voice and her demeanor caught my attention. I found an empty seat at the back of the room and listened.

I pulled out my notebook to scribble anything important she might say. Surprised at the first words I heard I knew I was in the wrong room. It did not matter. She spoke with authority, and somehow, I knew I needed what she was going to say. It was a funny little feeling in my gut that said, "Stay, listen!"

She said, "A good name is better than silver or gold, the Bible says. In Proverbs 22, it goes on to explain how there are rich and poor people in the world. Riches can come through hard work or by deceitful ways."

She stopped, looked in both directions, and taking a deep breath, she began again. "In verse four it says 'By humility and the fear of the Lord are riches, and honor, and life.' Thorns and snares are in the path of the unwise, but a wise person will be kept from these obstructions. Making wise choices will prevent the wise person from falling into the world's traps that will take a person down and steal their success."

I agreed with all that was said. She continued, "When we are young and full of vitality, we feel there is nothing that can stop us from succeeding at our goals. We often are overconfident in our own abilities, our own eyes. We have trouble seeing things realistically. Young people are idealistic, and that is good to a degree. It must be mixed with logic, experience, and wisdom, though. Here is where it pays to listen to your elders. They have gone through many of the things you, as a younger person, have not dealt with. You can learn from listening to them."

I knew this was true. I had been unstoppable in my younger years, but now things were beginning to change. She paused and then said, "Weigh all things in light of the Holy Scriptures. Advice comes from many directions, but you should always weigh that advice against the scriptures. If you are seeking success in your life, personal or business, weigh the advice against God's Word. Use only that which measures up to the Bible's wisdom. Get this understanding and you will be far ahead of the crowd.

Verse 6 of Proverbs chapter 22 says to 'Train up a child in the way he should go: and when he is old, he will not depart from it.' It is our responsibility as parents to train our children in God's word. A child will have a better life if you do this, and they choose to make their life decisions based on the Bible."

The speaker took a drink of water and cleared her throat. I was enjoying her talk and was glad I had stumbled into the wrong place. Putting the water bottle down, she said, "Listen carefully to the next verse. It is most important. Verse seven is a whole lesson on its own. The borrower is a servant to the lender. Jewish families recognized this early on and taught their children well. We can see in America today a total disregard for this biblical lesson. Most people are in debt, and they are a servant to the lender. They have to work hard to repay their loans. Credit cards are used like money, but they are not money."

She pulled a credit card from her pocket and held it up. She shook it to emphasize her point. "Credit cards come with huge interest rates if you do not pay back the entire balance every month. This interest is called usury in the Bible. Usury was a way for people to make money off other people and to become rich. The wise person saved their money and lent it out for a fee, the usury, or interest rate, as it is called today."

Sharing her personal experiences, she added, "When I was a young person, interest rates on credit cards were regulated by the government and could not go over a certain percentage. If they went over that, the companies could be fined or put out of business. As time went on, the interest rates became bigger and bigger. Politicians who make the laws, allowed the companies to charge more and more. Today, some rates are almost thirty percent. That means if you borrow one dollar, you pay back one dollar and thirty cents, and if you don't pay it back right away, that extra thirty cents gets added to the dollar you owe. Now you pay the thirty percent on the new balance, which includes the original principal and the interest you now owe. Interest continues to add up month after month, year after year until it is paid in full.

What a way to get rich! If only you had listened to that biblical principle in verse seven of Proverbs 22, you would not be in debt. You would not have to work so hard and be under such stress. The borrower is a servant to the lender. Don't be a borrower! Be a lender!

What happens when you don't or cannot pay? You lose the things you bought on credit to repossession. You lose your Good Name. You lose your good credit rating. You lose your position in your community, your self-identity, your self-worth. You feel worthless. Your good name was important, and you have lost good standing and brought shame on yourself and your family.

Being poor is not shameful, but being unwise is. People let their desires for things overcome their good judgment, and they buy things they cannot afford to pay cash for, on credit. It is so easy to put a credit card in the machine, and you feel you bought something. You get to take it home and use it, but it is not yours until it is paid for. Never forget this. Until you have paid in full, it is not yours.

Your friends may have the biggest and best play stations, videos games, cars, jewelry, clothing, or houses. They are blessed if they are paid for, but if they are using them while paying off loans and credit cards, they are under stress. The borrower is a slave to the lender.

How many parents have sat at the kitchen table and

explained this concept to their children? Not many, but the ones that do are usually the rich parents. They understand the meaning of these words, and they pass them on to their children. Poor parents continue to be unwise, and they never teach their children the things they need to know to be successful financially.

So, things never change. The rich become richer and the poor become poorer. 'A good name is rather to be chosen than great riches, and loving favor rather than silver and gold.' Read Proverbs, and learn to live in peace, and with prosperity."

With those last words, she closed her Bible and nodded at the audience. She walked off the stage, and the crowd applauded. People left the room, and I got to the door as quickly as I could. I walked into the hall and was standing there contemplating all that she had said. What a great message she had given, and I didn't even know her name.

I saw a hotel sign a few feet away and walked toward it to see if her name was printed there. There it was. As I read her bio, an older gentleman came up to me, and was expressing his gratefulness for the words she had just spoken. I agreed with him. Those were powerful words, and the message is something we need to share with others.

He told me he knew her when she was a young woman. They had been neighbors, and they had many talks on his front porch throughout the years. He had seen her grow in her faith, her understanding, and had watched her raise a family. I was intrigued and asked many questions.

He told me that wisdom comes a little at a time. If it is received, and it is watered and nurtured like a small plant, it will become a beautiful flower when it blooms. He said the speaker was now a mature bloom with petals to share. I thought, what a great analogy. We need to share the wisdom that we learn.

That was what the speaker was doing. I know it was no accident that I stumbled into that meeting. I was glad I missed the speech I was looking for, because I gained so much more. According to Psalms 37:23, 'The steps of a good man are ordered by the Lord: and he delighteth in his way.' And I know in my heart that my steps were ordered by the Lord that day.

Irresistible Cheese

Cheese, Cheese, Cheese,
Cut me a piece of cheese.
Yellow or white, creamy or brie,
I love cheese of all kinds.

It makes my sandwich better,
Makes my waistline fatter.
I don't care, fill my plate,
Cheese and crackers are my fate.

On veggies, or on meat,
The melted goodness heats,
Until it's gooey and it strings,
What a yummy taste it brings.

My mouth waters at the sight,
Of Cheese bubbling in oven light,
On Pizza, broccoli, or on chips,
Cheese finds its way to my lips.

Shapes of triangles, squares, or rounds,
Cheese in my fridge does abound.
Cheese tomorrow and today,
Cheese for me all the way!

Chicken Pot Pie

The sun was shining brightly, and the gentle breeze was making my sheets flip on the clothesline. Every time the wind blew, I could smell that wonderful fragrance of sunlight mixed with my favorite detergent. Line dried clothes smell so good. That is why I always hang my sheets on the line in my backyard when it is sunny.

"Hi there." The voice came from the neighbor's backyard. I looked up and saw the new lady that had just moved in next door. I had not had time to meet her and welcome her to the neighborhood.

"Hi. I'm Laura. Come on over." I pointed to my fence gate.

She smiled as she walked through the gate and held out her hand to shake mine. She said, "I'm Gloria. Just moved in."

"Yes, I saw the moving van and had planned to come visit you when I thought you were settled."

"We got most of the big stuff put away, but it will be weeks before I can go through all the small boxes. My husband went to work this morning and the kids are at school. I normally work, but I have the week off for moving."

"Well, that is just great. Won't you come in and have a cup of coffee with me?"

Gloria said, "Yes. I'd love that."

I poured two cups of coffee and offered a plate of cookies I baked yesterday. Gloria remarked how good the cookies were. I told her I used to bake all the time when my children were young, but now it is rare.

She said, "I never bake anything. My mom was always working, and she was tired when she came home. She didn't want me in the kitchen with her and we ate a lot of fast food while I was growing up. I guess I am doing the same thing to my kids now."

We both chuckled. I told her, "My mom died when I was young and my dad raised me by himself. We ate out a lot, too. When I got married, however, I decided to learn how to cook. I took a couple of cooking classes and that helped a lot. The best thing, though, was my aunt taking the time to show me little tips in the kitchen."

"Tips? Like what?"

"Well, tips like what you can substitute for different things if you don't have the best ingredients for a recipe."

"Really? You can do that?"

"Absolutely! I do it all the time."

"Wow," she said. It was like a light bulb came on in

her head. "I've not tried making lots of things in the past because I did not have the ingredients on hand."

"I'd be happy to show you a few things, if you'd like."

"Oh, yes!" she said with exuberance. "I've wanted some hands-on training for years and did not know who to ask. I felt so embarrassed, like I should know these things."

"Nothing to be embarrassed about here. I'd be happy to show you everything I know. But remember, I am not a gourmet chef or anything."

"Any help at all would be appreciated. I am so glad we moved next door!"

She got up and hugged me before she left. We promised to meet once a week on her day off and have a cooking lesson. I'm going to enjoy my new friend and neighbor.

*****

Two weeks passed before I saw her again. She rang my doorbell and asked if it was a good time. "Can we have a cooking lesson now?"

"Sure," I said. I was not busy at all. The timing was right. "Come on in."

We walked into my kitchen. I had placed some chicken thighs on the counter earlier to thaw. Chicken pot pie was on the menu for supper.

I said, "I'll show you how to make chicken pot pie."

"Oh, that sounds great! My family loves that, but I always buy the little ones at the grocery store. I just pop them in the oven, and it is easy."

"Yes, that's easy, but more expensive than the way I'm going to show you. Mine tastes better too, and it doesn't have any unnecessary ingredients."

We laughed. "I know preservatives and additives are bad. And I have been worried about feeding food with those things added to my family."

"First things first. Let's wash our hands and clean our counter." I washed my hands and handed her the bottle of hand soap. After cleaning the counter, I found my favorite tall pot to cook the chicken thighs in. I showed her how to always wash the chicken before cooking it. Putting it in the pot with water to cover, and adding salt and pepper, we let it boil until it was done. I told her if she was in a hurry, she could use canned chicken, but fresh was always better. I reminded her this was a substitute like we had talked about before.

"Gloria, today we are using a ready-made pie crust. At another time, I will teach you how to make pie crusts. Okay?"

"Sure, that's good for me. That will be super. My family loves pie and making homemade pie crusts would just be awesome."

She checked the chicken and gave it a stir. She was amazed at how rich the chicken broth was. "I never knew it was this easy to make chicken broth."

"Yes, easy. Always use chicken thighs with the skin attached. That has the fat you need and lots of vitamins. Now, let's remove the meat and cut it off the bone. Remove all the skin and cut the chicken into bite-size pieces. Put it in a separate dish."

She was actually having fun doing the work. It made me happy that I could help her and enjoy her excitement.

For the next step, I pulled a large mixing bowl from the cabinet. "This is a simple process," I said. "Put one can of mixed vegetables, drained, one can of cream of chicken soup, and half a can of chicken broth in this bowl, and mix it."

Gloria was a natural and enjoyed working with me in the kitchen. She shared a lot about her life, and I did as well. We were fast becoming good friends.

"Okay, now what?" she asked. "Is it time to put the chicken in?"

"Yes, you can do that, but first, let's chop a few onions and celery. We will put them in this little skillet with a tablespoon of oil for a few minutes. When they are almost soft, we will add them to our mixture."

Gloria took the skillet from my hand and in no time had the onions and celery ready to add to the mixing bowl.

"Now, it is time to add some garlic powder, some more salt and pepper, and any other spices you might like. I use a little poultry seasoning. It has several spices mixed in already."

After that, we put the mixture into the pie crust shell and topped it with another pie crust. I let Gloria crimp the edges and make slits in the top crust. We baked at 375 degrees for an hour, and it was golden brown. The aroma filled my whole house.

Gloria and I had a wonderful conversation while the chicken pot pie baked. We were relaxing when my husband called and asked if I'd like to go out to eat this evening. He got a raise at work and wanted to try a new restaurant that had recently opened near downtown. I was happy to say, "Yes!"

Gloria went home with the chicken pot pie for her family's evening meal. She was ecstatic, and so was I. It feels good to share a little knowledge with someone. It made me feel useful and needed. Gloria is young enough to be my daughter, and I am so glad she moved next door. I am looking forward to the next cooking lesson.

Happy Customers are the Key

It was a day like any other day. Up at 6:00 am, prepare breakfast for my husband and kids, get dressed in between making lunches, clearing the table, putting dishes in the dishwasher, feeding the dog and the cat, making sure everyone met their rides to work and school. Now it was my time to get ready.

It was a good thing I did not need to be there before 8:00, or I'd never make it. I only had a five-minute drive to work, and that also helped. Once I got to the office, opened up, made coffee for the crew, set the agenda for the day, I could begin to look at my appointments.

Being in business for myself was rewarding, but it also was much more work than the average woman had to do. I needed to make sure our company made a profit, so I could afford to keep my employees working. They had families that depended on me and my company to help them put food on the table. It was a big responsibility I carried on my shoulders.

I often wondered if anyone ever thought about me, and this huge responsibility I did not take lightly. I had no time to think about such things. I just needed to get it in gear and get the job done.

I often told my employees to do the same. **Work**

while you are at work, and take care of personal things when you are off work. That is the way a successful company runs. The focus is on the customers, not on the employees. I know that goes against modern thinking when everything is geared toward the "Me" in any situation.

I remember signs in businesses long ago that read, 'The customer is always right.'

That thinking and response to customer complaints kept the customer coming back and doing business with a company. That meant the employees kept their jobs and their livelihoods. The company succeeded and built on a good reputation. Repeat business builds a business.

Therefore, my training always emphasizes how we can do a better job of making our customers happy with our products and services. I wonder how many entrepreneurs understand this simple concept? It is our motto, and any employee I have that puts themselves above our customers does not work for me very long.

I heard the door open and close. My bookkeeper walked in and grabbed a cup of coffee. The good morning messages were exchanged and then other employees began filing in. The office was getting busy. Time for me to get to my schedule and start meeting my obligations.

The day went as usual. I met with an untold number of people, made deals, made progress on other ones, and answered every question imaginable. I was pooped. My head was foggy, and my feet hurt. It was time to start home. I would need to drop by the market and pick up a few things for dinner, and I knew we were just about out of milk.

How I kept all these things in my head all day long, I will never know. My jobs were exhausting, but it was not something I could put on hold. If I could just get home before the kids, take off those excruciating shoes, spend five minutes in the bathroom, I'd be okay.

Here they came, excited to show me their school papers. Such a good job, I'd say as I hugged them and pulled out a cookie and some milk for a snack. "Now, go change your clothes and get your homework done before supper. We'll play a game tonight."

Those days were challenging, but I made it through, and today those kids are all grown up. I imagine their lives are a lot like mine were. Rushing, rushing, all the time. I have more time now that I am retired. I can't move the way I used to, and to take on that kind of responsibility seems so far away. It is hard to imagine I did all that when I was young. It seemed like nothing then.

Time flies and things change. One thing never changes. That is my point about good customer service. I would still tell younger entrepreneurs today, if you want a successful business, give good customer service.

Repeat business will build any business. Without it, you will not survive. Word of mouth advertising happens when you please your customers. No business can afford enough paid advertising to overcome bad word of mouth advertising. **Treat your customers like you would want to be treated and they will come back.** Sometimes, they may be in the wrong and you will have to take that loss. In the end, it will be worth it if you keep that customer.

They say a happy customer tells ten people about your business. But an unhappy customer tells fifty. How could you possibly overcome that? **Keep your customers happy and they will keep coming back.**

(Are you in business for yourself? Are you running a woman-owned business? Roughly four out of ten businesses in the U.S. are owned by women, and more than 1,800 new businesses were started every day last year by women. Women entrepreneurs are responsible for a large percentage of job growth in this country. Women entrepreneurs are to be celebrated for their continued achievement.)

Real Estate Career

Real estate was my game,
Retired now, not the same.
Still have my license though,
But sales, have none to show.

Don't want to fight it anymore,
Appointments and unlocking doors.
People were different and it was fun,
Now, I just sit outside and enjoy the sun.

Do whatever I want to do,
Eat lunch and take a nap or two.
Ringing phones, and problems galore,
Made me often hit the floor.

No one had time to turn around,
Everyone talking became a blaring sound.
Forty plus years I endured the grind,
Now I have time to ease my mind.

Time to write and to share,
All the things, good or bad I bared.

It is fun to look back now and then,
See who I was way back when.

A broker with agents under me,
Responsible for what others see.
What was said and what was done,
Was all on me, under the gun.

Now I write about all those things,
Looking back, all the memories it brings.
I sometimes miss my old life,
But then again, gone is the strife.

Time to rest and enjoy my sleep,
Not well done when I was deep,
Into my career, I gave it all.
In small cotton, I'm standing tall!

Chapter 4
CHRISTMAS

Christmas Memories

Christmas Memories vary a lot from year to year. Living now as a senior citizen, I can attest to the ever-changing chapters of our lives. When I was a little girl growing up in a two-parent household, Christmas was the most spectacular time of year. The celebrations were well planned, with special decorations at every house. And the food was marvelous and brought from different households. The turkey and dressing was made at our house, though.

I could smell those delectable pies, cakes, and cookies made ahead of Christmas day every time I walked into my house. Days passed before we could sample the wonderful goodies hidden under or inside cake domes and Tupperware containers. If you visited the neighbors' houses or relatives' homes, it was the same way. Cooking was appreciated, and good cooks were held in high regard. Every woman tried to outdo herself year after year.

One of my favorite things was the homemade marshmallow fudge. My mother made it a month before Christmas and we sampled a little every night. The chocolaty goodness melted on our fingers, and we picked up every crumb that dropped from our grasp. The pecans in it were so good. Maybe it was because we gathered them in the Fall and shelled them on the front porch so mom could have them for the fudge.

I watched my mother pull those beloved recipes from the small indexed box that sat on the kitchen counter. There was a world of delicious meals and treats written on those recipe cards. She said, one day I would inherit that box. I treasured the thought of my mother's recipes being mine, and of me preparing Christmas traditions for my family.

The Christmas tree was decorated with colored balls and ornaments of every shape and size. Silver icicles were splashed on the end of every branch. My brother and I had that job and we loved doing it. It was tempting to splash a few on his head, and that happened once or twice, as I remember. We sang Christmas carols as we helped decorate the tree.

My dad brought home some stencils and aerosol snow we could spray on the windows. It looked so pretty from the outside. My brother and I loved those snow pictures on the windows. There were snowmen, Christmas trees, sleighs, reindeer, and one with Santa. When anyone walked by our house, our windows screamed Christmas! It was an exciting time, and in some years, a few days before the big event, it would snow. That was even better; a white Christmas!

Christmas Day finally arrived. My brother and I had many presents under the tree. We had to wait for our aunt and uncle to arrive before we got to open the gifts. It was hard, but Mom always offered us a piece of fudge to make the waiting less difficult.

Auntie and uncle came bearing gifts. The tree was overshadowed by the amount of presents under it. The first one I opened was the big three-foot baby doll I had wanted for months. She was so pretty and she could walk with me. I walked that doll all over the house and outside down the sidewalk.

What fun we had at Christmas time. My parents were not rich, but they never spared the expense at Christmas. It was always a day to remember.

As I grew older, it seemed Christmas excitement diminished a little. The belief in Santa was gone, and Christmas just became another secular holiday in my household. The celebration of Jesus Christ's birthday was never mentioned. Sure, we saw a few nativity scenes and heard the story, but it was not a part of our lives.

My parents did not attend church and saw no reason that my brother and I should go, either. I married and started my own family. Wanting a different way of life, I insisted that my husband and I attend church and rear our children in Christian ways.

Chapter two of my life had begun. It was not long

before I learned how to become a Christian and my whole life changed. My family was not happy about it, and they let me know. Eventually, they accepted my decision, but vowed never to change their way of life.

Christmas celebrations occurred at my house. I did the decorating, the cooking, the clean-up; I did it all before long. There was little help offered, but I did not mind. My children were important, and I wanted them to experience the excitement of Christmas I had as a child. I also wanted them to experience the miracle of Christ's birth. Jesus was the reason for the season, and our celebrations had to emphasize that.

One of my favorite Christmases was the year the boys both received new bikes. They had such fun with the new wheels that gave them the run of the neighborhood. Our house was the meeting place for neighborhood friends to congregate. Baking sweet treats for the children was something I loved doing. Christmas was a time of sharing and showing care to those less fortunate. I tried to instill these ideals in my boys. We spent time and money doing for others as well as doing for ourselves. Christmas with my boys was the best time of the year.

Chapter three of my life came sooner than I expected. I was a grandmother of five within a three-year period. Oh, my! What changes being a grandmother does to your life. I had little ones again in my home from time to time. Diapers, bottles, and sleepless nights were mine again. With five children under three, there was always lots of work to do.

When Christmas came, it was easier picking out toys and clothes. The children were all about the same size and liked the same things. So, I often bought five of everything, and the shopping was done.

I remember those little ones crawling on the floor and being hidden under a pile of Christmas wrapping papers. They had more fun with the torn paper than with the toys. They loved playing together, and those are sweet memories.

Watching them grow into teenagers was scary for this grandmother. I had no control over them, and I could only give advice occasionally. I prayed for them a lot. The world had changed drastically since I was that age, and not in a good way. The temptations were many, and peer pressure was strong. I could only hope and pray they would choose the right way, the Christian way.

Soon, they were grown and making a living, having relationships, getting married, having children of their own. How did this happen so quickly? I must be old. Chapter four is here and I am living it. A great grandmother is a wonderful name I cherish. Most of my grandparents were gone by the time I was born, so I cherish the time I have to spend with my grandchildren and great grandchildren.

Christmas is different now, but the excitement for the Savior's birth is still there. The excitement of Santa bringing gifts wore off long ago. Heavenly things will always remain while earthly celebrations lose their appeal. Our culture is slowly changing, and what was important to people when I was growing up is no longer important to today's younger people. It is sad for my generation to see this, but the younger ones don't even realize what they have lost. They probably think theirs is the better way.

I still have my mother's recipe box and I doubt any of my family will want those old recipes. Very few of the women even cook any more. Fast food restaurants, convenience, and fast-paced living have taken away age old traditions. It is sad, but a truth most of the baby boomers must acknowledge.

Looking back stirs the emotions and a tear finds its way down my cheek sometimes. Then I brush it off and smile. Thinking about all the lovely memories, I must say, "What a good life I have lived!"

Love Heals

"Christmas is coming!" her little sister yelled as she ran up the steps and into the apartment. Chris didn't care. Christmas had lost its meaning a long time ago for this cold-hearted young fourteen-year-old. Her innocence was taken away many years ago when her mom's boyfriend pushed himself on her while mom was working.

Chris had a bad attitude, and nothing, and nobody was going to change that. She was looking out for number one, and anyone who got in the way would get hurt.

Most of the people in the neighborhood knew Chris quite well. Many had seen her temper flare, and young children were kept at a distance. But those who dared became caught up in whatever maliciousness Chris dreamed at the time.

Vandalism and robbery were already on her police record. Beat cops knew her well. Some tried to befriend her, but others used her in various ways.

"Chris, come in here," her grandmother yelled as she leaned out the window of the apartment. Chris waved her off, but she kept yelling. People were looking at the commotion, so Chris shrugged and went toward the apartment.

"Young lady, it's time you got in here and ate your supper," Grandmother said.

"I'm not hungry."

"You quit smoking those cigs and you will be hungry!" Grandmother shot back.

Chris sat down at the table and pushed her food around on the plate. It was a hot meal, though made with meager ingredients. "This is crap! I don't want this!" Chris shouted and jumped up from the table and left the apartment.

Grandmother shook her head and tears fell from her eyes. She didn't know what to do to help her granddaughter. Her mom was no help, in and out of relationships, in and out of jobs, in and out of the apartment. Grandmother was tired and ready to give up when she heard a knock on the door.

She opened the door, and a young woman stood there with a smile on her face. Grandmother immediately did not trust her. Nobody in this neighborhood ever smiled. "What do you want?"

"Hello, I'm Maggie Strom. I'm your new neighbor across the hall, and I wanted to introduce myself."

"Nobody introduces themselves in this neighborhood, lady."

"Well, I just thought it was the polite thing to do." She held out her hand to shake.

Grandmother had not shaken hands with anyone in a long time and thought it was very strange, but she was compelled to do it, anyway. Her frank attitude had not changed Maggie's smile, and Grandmother found herself returning the favor.

"Won't you come in? Want a cup of coffee?" Grandmother asked.

"Why yes, that would be very nice," Maggie responded.

The conversation lasted a lot longer than either lady expected. Maggie explained her financial circumstances had taken a toll when her husband died, so she needed to relocate to a less expensive neighborhood. She was a counselor, and looking for a job. Grandmother gave her the name and number for the local community outreach, and Maggie said she would check it out the next day.

When Maggie left, Grandmother had a calm about herself. Maybe it was a slight ray of hope. "That's it, a ray of hope in the darkness."

Maggie met the people in her complex one at a time, but Chris watched from afar. She did not want to know the new neighbor and new counselor everyone was raving about. *She can keep her smiles and great attitude away from me.* Chris didn't like it that Maggie was affecting the neighborhood's children. Many were getting involved in sports, and her little sister was now even singing in a community choir. *What is this neighborhood coming to?*

Grandmother was telling Chris one day she should meet Maggie.

"Why would I want to do that?" She grabbed her jacket and headed for the front door, just as Maggie knocked. Chris opened the door, and Maggie stood there smiling.

"Well, Chris! I've been wanting to meet you," Maggie said.

"Hey look, I'm busy. Just on my way out the door."

"Well, so am I. I just stopped by to see if your grandmother needed anything from the store. I'm walking, so I can walk with you, too."

Chris shrugged and frowned. She didn't say a word, but Maggie came behind, still talking. She would not stop talking. Chris was aggravated. She was running away from everything Maggie was saying, but Maggie persisted.

"Chris, you can't run away all your life. You have to face things that hurt sometimes."

"You don't know anything about my life!" Chris blurted out.

"I know you are a hurt little girl inside, and you want to hurt back because you were hurt."

The truth stung, and Chris broke. She sat down on the corner bench, and tears welled up in her eyes. Defiant, she refused to cry. Maggie said, "It's okay to cry. Let it out. Holding it in only hurts you more. Don't you see that?"

Maggie sat down and moved close, putting her arm around Chris. Chris leaned her head over onto Maggie's shoulder. Years of built-up hurts came flowing out. No one paid attention to what was happening on the street corner. Maggie told Chris things she needed to hear and promised Chris she would be there for her. Chris received a lot of healing that day. It was like a miracle.

Today, Chris shares her story of how love healed her hurts. She says Maggie was just the instrument that God used to get through to her. To let her know that someone out there truly cares.

When hurts build up, we put up walls that create more hurt and despair. Just the concern of one person can make the difference in someone's life, and Chris encourages people to take the time to reach out to those that often turn you away. They really don't want to push people away, but fear, anger, and a distrust for others cause them to remain untouchable.

Chris is studying to be a counselor like Maggie. She wants to help others. She realizes that true happiness comes from helping others; such a difference from the narcissistic attitude she once held.

This Christmas will be much better, even without a lot of presents. Chris is determined to share the greatest gift-the gift of love.

How Christmas Was Saved

It was the first of December in our little up north town. The mayor was pacing the floor. Where was the Christmas tree for the town square? The workers usually had brought it by Thanksgiving. Where were they? The mayor was worried.

The mayor's assistant was busy typing a letter to a credit card company on behalf of the town, not being able to pay their bills. Like all the other town residents, money was tight and depression was visiting everyone.

With the virus spreading all over town, people are afraid to congregate. Would there even be a Christmas this year? Everyone was thinking the same thing. Inflation and supply chain issues are depressing, and the virus is scary. How will people stay six feet apart and gather around the Christmas tree on the town square? Will everyone wear masks to protect each other? Will the tree even arrive before Christmas? Would there be any Christmas joy this year?

Questions, questions, and concerns were on the minds of everyone. Jr. Stubblefield, or Junie, as he was often called, walked right into the mayor's office without knocking.

"Hey, mayor! What's up?"

"Junie, what are you doing here? Don't you know you're supposed to knock? I could have a meeting going on."

"Don't get your feathers ruffled," Junie replied. "I've got good news. The workers are on their way to town with the biggest, most beautiful tree you've ever seen!"

"Wonderful news, Junie! How did you find out?" the mayor said.

"I've got my ways." Junie strutted out the door.

The mayor breathed a sigh of relief. The town had money troubles, but at least the Christmas tree would be up on the town square shortly. Citizens could decorate it with their homemade decorations like every Christmas before, and everyone would gather round and sing Christmas carols. This might be a great Christmas after all.

Crash! Crash! Bang! Bang! The loud noise startled the mayor. He ran to the window to see what was happening. It was the truck carrying the Christmas tree. "Looks like the brakes failed on that old jalopy," his assistant said, pointing to the window as she walked into the room.

The mayor exclaimed, "They've run into the bank building!"

"Let's go see."

By the time the mayor and his assistant got to the scene of the crash, lots of people had gathered. Some were coming in and out of the bank building, looking at all the damage.

Others were attending to the driver and his helper. Fortunately, nobody was injured. Others were gasping at the tree!

That big, beautiful Christmas tree was broken in two. Yes, halfway down the trunk, the tree was broken. Like a dead puppy, it lay on the street, broken limbs and branches, bruised and cut in half. What would the town do now?

The mayor put his hands on his head in disbelief. His assistant began to shed tears. Men, women and children looked at the tree and a feeling of hopelessness engulfed the whole place.

"Looks like Christmas is a bust this year," said one man.

"Nothing good to see here," said the baker as he walked back to the bakery.

The lady that drives the taco food truck came to see for herself. She immediately started crying and wailing. This was not like her. She normally was a very happy person, but inflation had ruined her business, and this was the last straw.

Old man Hughes, that sits in a wheelchair, pushed his

way through the crowd. Despair lined his face. Even the children in the crowd slumped their shoulders as they turned to walk away.

One by one, the town's people came to pay their respects to the broken Christmas tree. This had been a tough year for everyone. It seemed like all good things had left and only despair remained.

Later that evening, Junie came along with his best pal, Dugger, and his dog, Peppy. The sight of the broken tree that had been left lying in the street saddened the three friends. It seemed like nobody had any ideas that could help.

Dugger said, "Hey Junie, if nobody cares, why don't we take the top of the tree and put it on a platform? It will be a small tree, but it is still a tree. It can reach up to the heavens like a big tree."

Junie smiled from ear to ear. "What a great idea!"

The boys built a platform while Peppy ran back and forth, watching the activity. Peppy wagged his tail with every nailed piece coming together. Soon, the platform was finished, and the boys attached the top of the tree.

"Good job!" Dugger said.

"Yeah, glad I thought of it."

"Hey, it was my idea!"

Peppy barked at the boys, and they stopped the argument.

"It looks naked," Junie said. "Let's go get some

ribbons and start decorating."

Dugger agreed. Both the boys found ribbons, and Dugger found some beads at his house. They came back and surrounded the tree with beautiful red and gold ribbons. They crisscrossed the colors and looped every limb. Dugger's beads were green and white and they stood out brightly. The street lamp lighted up the tree from top to bottom. It was a beautiful sight.

Peppy was so excited he chased the boys round and round the tree. The boys ran circles around the base of the tree while laughing at Peppy. Before long, the commotion alerted the town's people. The boys' smiles and bursts of laughter were contagious. There was a feeling of happiness not felt for a long time.

When the people saw the ribbons and beads, they gathered Christmas balls and bows from their homes. Many came running back, eager to be a part of the decorating. Soon, the tree was sparkling with gorgeous decorations from every family in town.

The baker brought a big cookie made in the shape of a star and placed it on top of the tree. It was sprinkled with sugar that glistened in the lamplight.

The taco food truck lady opened her truck for business and people bought tacos. Old man Hughes rolled over to the truck and Mrs. Page gave him a taco she had just purchased. He was surprised and gave her a big smile.

Everyone participated, and the tree represented every person, young and old. The mayor came out to see the tree. His assistant came too and wrapped a garland of popcorn on the branches.

He exclaimed, "What a miracle! This tree looks so lovely because it is decorated with love."

The townspeople clapped loudly and shouted in agreement. It would be a great Christmas after all.

"It is the Christmas spirit that is important, not the size of the tree," Junie said.

The mayor put his arm around Junie and his other arm around Dugger and thanked the boys publicly for their foresight in saving the tree and saving Christmas.

Dugger said, "Don't forget about Peppy. He helped too!"

The people laughed. When the church bells rang, everyone knew the Christmas season had begun. It was a time to be thankful for all that God had provided. The year had been hard, but they had survived. Thankfulness replaced the despair. Christmas carols became melodies of gratitude, reaching high into the air. Joy sprang up in each heart as Christmas time had arrived!

Christmas On Hold

As Julie prepares to get off the school bus, she has to walk past Marcie and Darla. The two girls look down at Julie's shoes and snicker. They are making fun of her tennis shoes. Julie is dreaming of the latest fad shoes, Strapperz. All the popular girls are wearing them, but they come with a hefty price tag. Julie's parents cannot afford such things, but Christmas is coming. Maybe, just maybe, she will get lucky this year.

The days are getting colder, and the leaves are falling on the ground. The first snow is scheduled to arrive this weekend. Mom prepares a skillet dinner for the family meal tonight. She adds a little more garlic powder and some fresh chopped onions to make it tastier.

Julie opens the backdoor and slinks into the kitchen. "Hi, Mom. What's for dinner?"

"It's on the stove. We're having a salad and some garlic bread too."

"Looks good. I love this stuff and I am so hungry. Lunch at school today was so bad, I couldn't eat it."

"Now, Julie. You've got to eat lunch. You can't do good work if you don't eat lunch."

"I know, Mom. I tried a little of everything, but it all

tasted awful."

"Well, go get washed up. Dinner will be ready as soon as I get the salad prepared. Tell your brother to wash up too."

"Sure thing, Mom." Julie hurried off to her room.

"Joe, dinner is almost ready," Mom yelled from the kitchen window. Her husband was outside wrapping the water hydrants for winter.

"Almost done. Be right in," Joe replied.

Everyone agreed the dinner was delicious. The conversation was delightful, and Mom felt proud of herself. She loved pleasing her family with a good hot meal and to hear her loved ones' experiences of the day made her feel accomplished. Motherhood is hard at times, but dinners like tonight made it all worthwhile.

Joe said he'd clean up the dishes tonight while Mom took a long hot bath. She was surprised at his thoughtfulness. This was just the best day ever!

Mom put lavender bubble bath liquid in the hot water and, as she was soaking, she dreamed about Christmas. It would be here before long and she liked to plan ahead. She had already started stocking up on baking essentials for the extra cooking she always did for relatives and neighbors. It was a yearly ritual.

She needed to find out what her husband wanted for Christmas. He was the one that was hardest to buy for. The kids always needed new clothes, electronic gadgets, and toys. They were easy to buy for. It was Joe that required more thought.

She had put away an extra couple hundred dollars, but she would need much more. Inflation was killing her budget these days. Just going to the grocery store costs twice as much as last year. When will the prices stop rising? She wondered how much more the American people could take. She had not told her husband, but the past two weeks the groceries were bought with a credit card.

Joe would be angry if he knew that. He always told her credit cards are only to be used in an emergency. Well, if buying groceries is not an emergency, she doesn't know what is.

Hopefully, she can catch up in a month or so. She has been watching the little extras and not buying some things she normally buys. Still, she is losing ground. She needs to save more for Christmas, but if things do not go back down in price soon, there will be no extra money.

She worries a little, but tonight's bubble bath is too comforting to worry very much. *That husband of mine is pretty wonderful*, she thought.

Joe and the kids were off the next morning, and Mom put on her business outfit and headed to her part-time job. She only had to work five hours today and that would give her some extra time to go window shopping. She had seen an advertisement for power tools at the hardware store. She thought maybe she could find a bargain and something Joe would really like. Sure enough, the sale was twenty-five percent off and the combo she picked out would be something he could use and something he would really want. Without the money to buy, she put it on lay-a-way. She had almost two months to pay it off. Lay-a-way was a tool she had used for years to get a bargain when she didn't have all the money up front. It had worked great in prior years.

Mom was on top of her game. Joe was taken care of, and now picking out the kids' presents would be easy. She knew most everything they wanted could come from Shopper's World and she could put a deposit down on a lay-a-way plan.

The only other thing she needed to buy was a pair of Strapperz shoes for Julie. She went to the department store for those. When she turned over the price tag, it made her hand shake. She looked at the tag for a few moments and swallowed hard. Of course, the shoes were not worth the cost, but her daughter wanted those shoes so badly.

It was Christmas. She would just have to tighten the budget a little more, because the shoes were important to Julie. She knew how important after she accidentally overheard a phone call with Julie and her best friend. Julie was crying and telling her friend how some of the other girls were teasing her.

Within a week or two, all the gifts were tucked away in bins at the stores waiting for final payments. Mom took a few more hours at her part-time job and asked for more. The company could not give any more, however. They said sales were down, and they just didn't need any more help. She was lucky to get the hours she had been given.

Thanksgiving came and went. It was a great weekend of family, friends, and football. Everyone enjoyed themselves, but Mom was exhausted with all the cooking and the guests. Mom was glad when Monday came and everyone went back to school and work. She said she could finally get some rest.

That evening, Joe came home with a very sad face. "What's wrong, honey?"

"Sit down," he said. "I have some very bad news."

Joe told her he had been laid off from his job. The company had financial troubles and supply issues. It could not come back. They were closing up the facility. Management was moving out of state, but all the workers would just have to fend for themselves.

"Oh, no! How can this be? They've been the heart of this community for decades!"

"I know, honey. We were all surprised. Nobody in my section knew about any of this until today."

"What are we going to do, Joe?"

"Unemployment insurance; we will file for

unemployment."

"Yeah, but we are barely making it now. Unemployment is not enough."

"Honey, it will have to be enough."

Mom started to cry thinking about the mortgage, the higher utility bills, the price of gasoline, it was all up in price. Their income was down and the cost of living was up. It had just been announced taxes were rising too. Then, Mom remembered the Christmas gifts on lay-a-way. How would she finish paying for them?

Was Christmas going to be ruined this year?

Mom decided not to tell Joe about the Christmas gifts on lay-a-way. He had enough to worry about right now. During the next few days, she got busy baking cakes, cookies, and making candy to sell to neighbors. She baked and baked and the sales even surprised Mom. However, the sales were not adding up to the amount of money needed to get everything out of lay-a-way.

Julie was a big help at delivering the orders after school. She did not know for sure why Mom had started the baking, but she had an idea the family really needed the money. She had heard Mom and Dad talking one night about the bills and the fact that the unemployment payments had not started coming in yet. Dad was frantically searching for another job, but so were the other laid-off workers.

One day Julie was delivering cookies to Mrs. Smith,

the elderly neighbor on the next street over. Mrs. Smith asked Julie to have a seat on the porch and gave her a glass of milk, and offered her a cookie she had just bought from her.

Mrs. Smith had no children of her own, and she said she would appreciate the company. They had a great visit. Mrs. Smith ordered more cookies and every time Julie delivered them, they had another visit with milk and cookies.

Julie told Mrs. Smith about her dad losing his job. She said her mom was worried about Christmas. Julie had heard her parents discussing the lay-a-ways, and knew her mom would be sad if she could not get them out before Christmas. In fact, the store policy was to re-stock everything that was not picked up by Christmas. The shopper would lose any deposits they had made. This was the reason Julie was so happy to help sell and deliver the baked goods.

Mrs. Smith said, "I see. Well, your mom's baking has helped me a great deal."

Julie was happy to hear that. She had enjoyed visiting with Mrs. Smith and sharing cookies and milk with her. When she left, she only had to go two doors down to deliver a cake before she headed back home.

The next day, mom was rolling out pie crusts when the phone rang. It was Shopper's World customer service. They asked when she would be picking up her lay-a-way. She swallowed hard and said, "I'm not sure. I don't have enough money yet to pay it off."

"Oh no," the clerk said. "Your bill is paid in full. I just need to know what time you will be picking up your merchandise."

"What? Paid in full?"

"Yes, ma'am. Paid in full. What time will you be here?"

"Twenty minutes. I'll be there in twenty minutes." Mom laid down the phone and could not believe her good fortune. Had Joe paid it off with money she did not know about? She would find out when he got home, but she needed to get to the store.

Mom rushed home with the gifts and quickly hid them in various spots throughout the house. She wondered where Joe got the money. About that time, the phone rang again. It was the hardware store, asking when she could pick up her merchandise. How did Joe know about this? It was a surprise, and she had not mentioned it to him.

She grabbed her purse and keys and was headed to the car when a delivery truck from the department store pulled up in front. The delivery man asked her to sign and gave her a package. It was Julie's shoes. Mom was stunned. How was this happening? Joe was out looking for a job, and she could not call him. She had to wait until he got home, but she had to hide this important package now. After hiding the shoes, she hurried to the hardware store to pick up Joe's gifts.

The afternoon was spent hiding and re-hiding gifts. Mom needed to make sure nobody found the gifts before Christmas Day. She didn't know how this miracle happened, but she was so thankful. When everything was put away, Mom went back to her baking. She made six pies and three dozen cookies.

Her good fortune made mom realize how rich her family truly was. She wanted to give back to others. When Julie got home, mom loaded her baskets with the baked goods and told Julie to deliver them but not to charge the people any money. It was her gift to them.

Mrs. Smith was pleasantly surprised by Julie's mom's generosity. She told Julie good deeds always come back to you. Julie said she didn't understand how her mom could work so hard and give away her baked goods when she needed the money so badly. Mrs. Smith smiled and said, "Maybe she doesn't need it as badly now as she did before."

Julie looked puzzled and said, "Yeah, maybe not."

Mrs. Smith said, "Julie, Christmas is not about presents, but it's about sharing love and what God has given us."

Julie smiled and nodded as she left Mrs. Smith's house. She had a happy, peaceful feeling inside. Julie knew her mom was sharing Christmas love, and she was a deliverer of that love. She did not know how Mrs. Smith was involved, but she had a hunch she was a part of it, too.

Christian Comedian

Christian Comedian, where have you gone?
Laughing at your words, and your songs.
You were so crazy and so much fun,
Audience was captured until you were done.

You came from a long way off,
To our little town, sick with a cough.
But it did not stop you from going on stage,
Jumping right in, laughter filled the place.

Your jokes were wild and almost shocking,
Laughed so hard when you were mocking.
Years before, in the world, you did hang,
You smoked dope and ran with a gang.

Now, here you were, saved and cleansed.
You knew the way of worldly men.
But you chose to follow Christ, give it all up
To live your life holy, the sin you dumped.

A Christian Comedian, we all need today.
Where did you go? Why did you go away?
We need some laughs and giggles more,
When way back then, we were not as sore.

Come back and play your gig again,
Because Laughter is the best medicine.
We need to laugh and rest from worries,
Hear clean jokes that are not blurry.

Christian Comedians, stand up once more.
I promise audiences will flock to your door.
Come out of the shadows, let God use you,
Your gift lifts the spirit and breaks the blues.

Speak up, and speak funny, exaggerate if you must,
But don't use foul language that always disgusts.
The world is your stage someone once said,
God will give you jokes, if Holy Spirit led.

I am sure God laughs at us,
And He loves when we have fun.
Doing things that are not sin,
Making merry and honoring Him.

So, make your life as pleasant as can be,
Smile and laugh, enjoy each other's company.

Christian Comedians have a special place,
God puts them at top of the human race.

Christian Comedian, come laugh with me,
Joy and happiness, I love to see.
Humor can change a person's life,
As easy as a rolling tide.

Chapter 5
Cousin Annie

Visiting Cousin Annie

About four decades ago, I would visit my mom's cousin, Annie and her boys, for two weeks every summer. Sure Shot Annie was her nickname because she was so accurate when shooting her shotgun. I was a couple of years older than Buster, and Little Butch was just like a little brother to me.

I thought they had the finest life of all. Being a city girl, it was all new and fun to me. I did not mind feeding animals or cleaning rabbit pens to help out. Milking goats was fun to watch, but I just couldn't get the hang of it. I sure did like the taste of Cousin Annie's homemade ice cream, made from goat's milk. Nothing tasted like her sweet desserts.

Summertime on the Stone Ranch was fun, after all the chores were done. Feed the animals, clean the pens, hang the wash on the line, and go out to the creek with a picnic lunch. The rock bedded limestone creek only ran during the Spring and early Summer. As the days got hotter, the water dried up. It was only a run-off creek. While there was still water, it made a fine place to dip your feet or take a bath.

The beautiful, bright yellow sunflowers covered the field behind the creek. The purple verbenas made a contrast along the border of the field. But, by far, the prettiest part was the hillside covered with bluebonnets. Every Spring, the
bluebonnets covered that hillside just like a blanket of blue. There were a few coral pink Indian paintbrush, and red and gold Mexican Hat mixed in.

The colors were vibrant on a clear, sunny day, and the flowering plants made the whole area smell like perfume. You could become intoxicated by the smells coming from the creek area. Sometimes, I would lie in the flowers and get pollen all over my body. I looked like I'd been dusted with cornmeal.

Most days, we raced to the creek. Whoever got there first got an extra helping of fried chicken. That picnic basket with the grease stained, red checkered cloth inside was full of finger licking good chicken. Cousin Annie was a great cook, and they had so many chickens running around, nobody missed one or two.

If you were the last one there, you had to sleep on the floor that night. They only had 2 beds besides Cousin Annie's. So, two of us got a bed and one of us got the floor. We learned to run fast that summer. We loved the creek. The water ran fast and cool. The days were so hot, the sweat poured, and the creek felt so refreshing. We took a bar of soap and Cousin Annie said, "You's might as well scrubb while ye's playing in the warter."

Cousin Annie and the boys talked funny. I guess it was a dialect problem in their county. My folks didn't much like to hang out with Cousin Annie, but they let me enjoy the summertime visits, alone. I bet they missed me while I was gone, and having so much fun.

My parents didn't like that kind of fun, they said. They used to call Cousin Annie "prime-a-tive". I thought they meant she was prime about something, probably being a sure shot and all. Today, I don't think that's what they meant.

Cousin Annie was a pretty smart woman, though. She had a trophy for shooting a rattlesnake. I saw a purse she made from the skin of that critter, and she offered to give it to me. My mom said I should not take such a fine prize from Cousin Annie. It just wouldn't be right.

Well, the best time we had that summer was Little Butch's birthday party. A lot of the neighbor's kids came and brought presents. The cake was scrumptious and topped with homemade ice cream. Cousin Annie loved making her boys happy with her divine cooking skills. We played games outside all afternoon. Those kids were a lot of fun.

When the party was over and the kids left, Cousin Annie brought out the best present of all. She gave little Butch a three-wheeler that year. He had begged for it ever since Toby, his neighbor friend, got one. Little

Butch just thought he had to have one, too. Cousin Annie saved and saved until she could make his dreams come true.

Cousin Annie knew it was a big responsibility, and Little Butch heard a lot of instruction concerning the three-wheeler. He promised not to let any other kid drive it. She gave him good training and watched him take it up and down the road. Little Butch practiced every day. He was allowed to drive it in the fields and on the trails. He could take Buster or me on the back of it, but we could not drive it. Only Little Butch was allowed to drive it, because he had the training and it was his property. He had the responsibility of owning a motor vehicle. Cousin Annie was a pretty strict parent. Little Butch knew he had to obey, or it would be taken away as fast as it came.

Cousin Annie went to the neighbor's farm one day to help a lady do some canning. While she was gone, Buster and Little Butch got into a tangle. I stayed out of it, but Little Butch left the house in a huff. He drove down the road on his three-wheeler. Buster and I got involved in a game of monopoly and never gave another thought to Little Butch.

Cousin Annie came home a few hours later and asked where Little Butch was, but we did not know.

"What? Ye's don't know wher's Little Butch is?"

We shook our heads. No, we had no idea where he

went.

Cousin Annie said, "I's gittin in da truck to go sees iffin I cud fine him."

That's when Dave, from down the road, drives up. Little Butch is in the front seat, holding his head. The three-wheeler is in the truck bed, not looking too good.

Cousin Annie said, "Dave, whut happen?"

Dave told Cousin Annie, Little Butch let Jimmy Sheary drive the three-wheeler. They rounded a bend in the road and Jimmy could not handle it. They went into the ditch and bounced back up on the other side. The three-wheeler was headed for a fence post. Jimmy leaned right and Little Butch's face hit that fence post smack down the center.

It was a good thing he did not move to the left or right because that was a four-strand barbed wire fence. Little Butch would have lost his head. Cousin Annie was so mad she was both yelling and crying. She hugged Little Butch and spanked him at the same time. Yelling, crying, he was in trouble, and his face was black and blue. She could not punish him too much, because she was so happy he was still alive.

The three-wheeler sat in the barn for the rest of the time I was visiting. Waited until the next summer to see if Little Butch's face ever healed up. He was a lucky dude!

Porchin' With Cousin Annie

Some of my favorite memories of the 1980s are of days I spent with Cousin Annie. The lessons I learned about life on her front porch have enriched me in ways I never dreamed possible. I was truly blessed to know her and have her as my cousin.

My Mom thought it was good for me to spend a few weeks each summer on Cousin Annie's farm. Mom did not like farm life or most anything about Cousin Annie. I don't know why she was ok with me enjoying my summer trips out there. I had a lot of fun with Buster and Lil' Butch, though. They were like my brothers. Being an only child living in the city was not as much fun as visiting Cousin Annie.

Buster and Lil' Butch got a part-time job from Mr. Gandy down the road during hay season. They saved that money for new school clothes, so I did not mind staying all day long with Cousin Annie while they made a little money. Seeing how dirty they were each evening after work, I was glad to stay home and help Cousin Annie with chores. I think I had the easier job.

One day, we sat on the front porch for half the day just shelling peas from the garden. I had never shelled peas before, but once you got the hang of it, it wasn't so bad. Next day, we snapped the green beans. Cousin Annie did a lot of canning that summer. She said the rains came at just the right time, and that is why the garden did so good that year.

Cousin Annie didn't talk much about my mom. I think she knew Mom did not appreciate her the way I did. I asked her why she liked living on the farm. She said there was peace out in the country, not like bumper-to-bumper city living.

"What do you mean bumper-to-bumper city living?"

"Awww, yous knows. People everywhere. Bumping into each other, no matter where ye's goes. Too many people. Too many cars. Too much noise. Don't like it much."

"Oh, so you like fewer people?"

"You might say dat."

"Don't you get lonely out here?"

"Why, darlin', no. We's has great neighbors and lots of friens at the church. We get together with people all the time. We's jus like a lil' elbow room."

With that, she picked up another bushel of green beans and brought them over to my rocking chair.

"More beans?" I asked.

"Yep, we's gotta do 'em all."

"Okay," I said, as I wiped my brow. It was getting a little warm on the porch. Cousin Annie said she would be right back. In a few minutes, she reappeared with two big glasses of iced tea with lemon. That was the bestest tea I'd ever drank. Cousin Annie said it was the clear spring water that made the difference, and I bet she was right.

We snapped and rocked and talked all afternoon. Rocking is something I still love to do. I guess I was the right age to learn a lot of things that are important in your older years. I kept a lot of Cousin Annie's old sayings, and I apply them to life today. She may not have been formally educated, but she was a wise woman.

I remember the day I asked her about boys and boyfriends. She said I was too young for all that, but I should know what to watch out for. Cousin Annie had a way of explaining things that made you feel sure you knew what she was talking about, but later you had to stop and rethink it. Maybe she did that on purpose. I think she did. I learned a lot of lessons from Cousin Annie and a lot about farm life and animals.

Cousin Annie taught me to cook and appreciate leftovers. She threw nothing away. She found a way to make leftovers appetizing. You never knew what would be for dinner, because it was different every night. The boys were clueless.

They never thought they had leftovers, but Cousin Annie and I would grin and kept the secret between us girls.

One morning Cousin Annie said, "Come on, sister. Get your apron on." Cousin Annie called me sister all the time. I don't know why.

She grabbed my hand, and we went running to the creek. There was a fence line down there that belonged to the neighbor. There were wild berries growing all along that line. She told me to hold my apron up and start picking.

"Oooh, look at this one."

She held up the biggest blackberry I'd ever seen. Then she pushed it into my mouth. Juice ran down my chin; it was so delicious and sweet. Blackberry juice was all over our clothes by the time we finished picking the berries. Cousin Annie and I raced to see which of us could fill our aprons the fastest.

It was hard because we kept eating the best ones. I think that was the most fun I had with Cousin Annie. She wasn't like most grown-ups I knew. She was fun to be with!

At home, Cousin Annie showed me how to make a pie crust from scratch. No mind a little flour on the floor, it would sweep up. She rolled out four crusts in no time at all.

Two were for the bottoms and two for the tops. We

washed those blackberries and had to cut some of them, because they were too big for a mouthful. We put them in the pie crusts and sprinkled sugar, a tablespoon of flour, dotted with butter pats, and added the always dab of cinnamon. Cousin Annie loved cinnamon and said never cook anything without a dab of cinnamon. I still use cinnamon like that today in remembrance of my great Cousin Annie.

Blackberry pie isn't the same anymore without Cousin Annie and the wild blackberries we gathered by the creek. But that memory is one of my best. I wish kids today could live what I lived back then. They would appreciate the little things in life more and realize maybe those are the "Finer Things in Life."

Cousin Annie Escapes
The Big Storm

When I was just a young girl, my parents took me to visit my Cousin Annie. Mom and Dad were going on a cruise and would be gone for three weeks. I had the joy of visiting Mom's cousin, Annie. Mom and Cousin Annie were as different as night and day. I suppose that is why I loved her so much. Cousin Annie was my favorite relative.

She lived way out in the country. It took a long time to get to her house. The cement of the city gave way to narrow roads lined with trees of every variety. The drive was long, and I used the time to imagine all the things we would do when I was there. Cousin Annie always taught me things I never would have learned in the city. It was a vacation I needed more than my parents needed the vacation they were taking without me.

Long winding roads continued, and before long there were the hills I loved in the foreground. We were almost there, and my excitement was growing. Cousin Annie would hear our car arriving, and she would meet and greet us from her front porch. Buster and Little Butch would be waiting, too. Lucy, their big collie dog, would run to me, jump up, and lick my face if I allowed her to do so.

Once we arrived, it was only a short while before Mom and Dad left, and the four of us dug into the blueberry pie Cousin Annie had made. She said she prepared it in honor of my visit. It made me feel special. She knew it was my favorite. The summer before, she taught me how to make one myself. I'll always be appreciative of the life lessons and skills Cousin Annie shared with me.

The warm days of summer meant swimming in the creek, going barefoot, and picking wildflowers for the table. It meant smelling chicken frying on the stove, sitting on the porch whittling, and lots of iced tea.

Buster and Little Butch took a long hike with me. Lucy came along and sniffed along the sides of the trail as we walked. The dog would run ahead of the three of us, but sometimes she would spend too much time sniffing a broken tree branch and we would get ahead. Lucy would come from behind and almost knock us over to get into the lead again. She was such a fun dog. I thought Buster and Little Butch had the perfect life.

Lucy was ahead of us several yards when she began barking at a rock. She was moving from side to side and jumping up and down, alerting us to the danger. We stood back and watched her. She continued to bark and look closely at the rock. She put her paw on it and jumped back. Buster was calling for her to come back to where we were. He was afraid she would get hurt, but Lucy would not stop and come back.

Finally, Buster told us to stay put, and he would slowly go forward and see what it was. Maybe it was a snake under the rock? He picked up a stick for protection if it struck at him.

Slowly, he stepped forward. Calming Lucy with his words. Lucy looking at him, then at the rock. As Buster approached, the look on his face changed from worry to delight. He started laughing, and looked at us and said, "Come over here."

He was laughing so hard. We ran to see what it was. A big ole turtle with dried mud over his back looked just like a rock. Lucy's barking must have deafened that poor turtle's ears. Little Butch reached down and patted Lucy's back. "Good dog, Lucy. You're a great hunter!"

We left that poor turtle and went on with our walk to the creek. I hoped Lucy would be as diligent with a snake as she was with that turtle. I was sure she would be. She pranced down the trail like a victorious warrior protecting her clan.

We skipped some rocks on the water, sat on the bank and talked about grown-up things. Buster and Little Butch had grand ambitions, and thought about world events more than I did. How strange that country kids were more involved in life's bigger issues than a city girl like me. I wondered why that might be?

Lucy got in the water and when she came out, she shook water all over us. That was when Little Butch said, "Enough. Let's get home." We all followed him back to the trail, and we ran the last quarter mile when we saw their house come into view.

Life was sweet in the country. The fresh air made the clothes smell wonderful when they were hung on a line outside to dry. The food tasted better since most of it was grown in rich fertile soil on their farm. Days were slow, and yet the time passed too quickly for me. I could stay here forever.

One day, Cousin Annie asked if I'd like to accompany her to the wild lettuce field below the hill. Of course, I was eager to go with her. She and I would have time to talk, and she had the best stories.

On the way there, she told me about the time her daddy had a tire blowout on the road to their house. The car swerved and landed in the ditch. The tow truck driver came and got the car out of the ditch. That was the first time she met her future husband. Annie married him six years later, and Buster and Little Butch were born after that.

I never knew Annie's husband, because he was killed years ago in a freak car accident. Buster and Little Butch were left without a father and cousin Annie became a widow. She managed the farm and the boys well. I deeply admired my cousin Annie.

We arrived at the wild lettuce field and were filling our buckets with the delicious green leaves. As we picked the plants, the sky became dark. Clouds were rolling in. We could hear thunder in the background. Cousin Annie said, "Pick faster. A storm is brewing, and we need to get all we can and get home before the rain comes."

"Yes, ma'am." My fingers were sore already from the little stickeries that were mixed in with the wild lettuce plants. I kept picking, though. It thundered, and I jumped. It felt like the earth shook.

Cousin Annie dropped her bucket, and it spilled. She began picking up the leaves and putting them back into the bucket. Another boom of thunder shook us again.

"It's coming fast. We better get home."

No sooner had the words come out of her mouth, but lightning struck a nearby tree. The sky lightened, blinding us for a few moments. The tree sizzled and then cracked. It was on fire and came crashing to the ground.

"Run to the hill!" she screamed at me.

I ran, hopping over the little trickle of a creek and up to the side of the rocky hill. There was a small cave on the hill there, and cousin Annie and I stood inside of the rock covering to avoid the rain. It was coming down hard. Cousin Annie's bonnet, she always wore, was soaked, but her hair was still dry. She took it off and squeezed the water out of it and put it back on her head. My hair was dripping, nothing I could do about it now.

The rain continued to pour down. Cousin Annie said we had no choice but to wait it out. We were getting splashed with the rain, so we stepped back further into the cave. With no light, we could not go back much further. We sat on the cave floor, resting, waiting out the storm.

A loud noise like a train came whistling into the cave. Cousin Annie looked at me, and that was the first time I'd ever seen fear in her eyes. "It's a tornado!"

She told me to get up and move deep into the cave. We hung onto the side wall of the rock cave and slowly made our way in the dark. Cousin Annie was in front of me, and as she stepped forward, her foot was covered in water. There was an underground lake inside the cave. We could go no further. We stopped and held onto each other until the loud noise of the tornado passed. My heart was beating faster than it had ever beaten before.

When the noise stopped, we inched back toward the entrance of the cave. The rain was still pounding the earth, and we could hear water rushing. The little narrow creek was now a rushing river. It was coming closer and closer to the entrance of the cave.

Water from the underground lake inside the cave was

also rising. The cave floor was being inundated with water. We were trapped in between both. Soon, the waters would rise more, and they would come together and we would be swept away. Cousin Annie said, "Leave your bucket. We've got to get out of here."

I looked at our buckets of wild lettuce sitting on the cave floor and water was swirling around the base of both buckets. They would soon be gone.

I followed Cousin Annie, and we left the cave and climbed up the hill one foothold at a time. It was straight up and down, not an easy climb. There were large areas of single, slick rocks where you could slide off if you were not careful. I was scared of sliding off and falling into the rushing creek, that was now turned into a river. No one would ever find my body.

Cousin Annie led the way. She was good at finding little indentions in the rock. Fortunately, the rain slowed, and it was easier to navigate the climb. Soon, we were at the top of the hill, and the rain stopped. We sat and looked down at the creek. It was amazing how quickly that calm little creek became a rushing river capable of major destruction.

Cousin Annie knew flash floods. She had escaped from many over the years. It was my first time and hopefully, I would not be that close to another one. Our wild lettuce trip was one I shall always remember, but I may never get to taste the delectable greens.

Danger, Danger Everywhere

Watch where you're walking!
Watch out for snakes,
Watch out for crooks,
Don't fall in the lake!

Life can be dangerous,
When you don't pay attention,
Watch out, watch out,
It's all stress and tension.

"No, it's not," my sister said,
"Who put those thoughts in your head?"
"It's the news I watch each day,
All the photos they show, and what they say."

"Turn the TV off, you silly girl,
Lots of good things in this old world.
Pay attention to what will lift you up,
Tell negative people to shut up.

Feed your body with healthy food,
Feed your mind with only good.
More productive and happy you'll be,
Concentrating less on what is mean.

Be aware and be prepared,
For we cannot control the times,
Living in the last days
There will be more crime.

We have a helper in our God,
Prayers to Him can protect our bods.
Talk to Him every day,
Never forget you need to pray.

Watch out for danger,
They spread on the news."
I'm blessed and richer in Jesus,
And with Him, I will not lose.

Chapter 6

Watch Out For Danger

It's A Twister, Mister

The Daily Esquire headlined the new shopping center coming into town. Within the year, ground would be broken. Chamber of Commerce was all abuzz. The planning and zoning board was holding regular meetings to answer questions the public had concerning the location. The newspaper was happy with the increased sales. They wanted to keep the news humming.

Doc Salvia knew it would mean more jobs for the community. That was important if he were going to convince his granddaughter to stay here after graduation from high school. She did not want to go to college, even though there was a community college in the next town. It was an easy drive, but she had other ideas. She wanted a job. Jobs in the big city paid more, but that was so far away. Doc had spent the past few months talking to her about the benefits of small-town living.

Sonderville was right in the middle of tornado alley. It was a fine town with great people, but jobs were scarce since the box factory closed five years ago. The school system, the city, and county offices were the largest employers. Even the small hospital had trouble staying open. Doc did not charge his patients as much as he could have if he lived in a larger town.

"Some things are more important than money," he would tell his granddaughter.

She would often answer him with, "You can't eat good will."

He knew he needed to help the council and the chamber come up with ideas to attract more business to Sonderville. If the town was going to survive, new businesses had to be added, and soon.

He was in deep thought as he drove home, and was not paying attention to the dark clouds gathering. As he passed the Farm Bureau and rounded the bend, the twister came across the road in front of him. He was traveling 55 miles per hour, and the twister was just a blur of debris that blocked his view for a few seconds.

It continued across the field to his right. It struck the corner of the Ramada Inn and bounced off and into the clouds. The wind left the bricks of the building piled high on the ground. The roof was torn away, and the rain poured in.

Doc wiped his forehead and blew out a sigh as the twister came out of nowhere. Only a few seconds, and it was gone. Shaken a bit, he decided to stop at the grocery for a few things. It would give him a chance to stop the car and thank God he was not touched by the twister.

"Twisters! Darn those things! You can't get ahead in this town. You build something and the dad-blasted wind comes and tears it up!" the old grocery man was saying as Doc walked in.

"Hey, did you see that twister hit the motel?" Doc asked.

"See it? Yeah, I felt it. I thought it was going to take out my windows!"

"Good thing it didn't. I need some milk."

"Aisle 7, by the ice cream."

"Yes, I know where it is."

Doc walked on back to pick up some milk and thought, why not get some ice cream too? That grocery man knew the power of suggestion.

Now, if only he could persuade his granddaughter not to move, as easy as the grocery man persuaded him to buy ice cream. His thoughts were consumed every day by this. It meant a lot to him, since she was his only relative left in this town. Her parents' car accident years before, left big holes in the family unit. What would he do if his granddaughter left this town, too?

He had been a stellar citizen in this community. Being the only doctor in the area way back when he first arrived, he had prominence. Everyone knew Doc Salvia, and his words and ideas held weight. Why couldn't his granddaughter build on his legacy? Why did she want to go someplace where she knew no one? It did not make sense to Doc.

"Hey, Doc. Is this all you need?" the grocer said as he rang up the bill.

"Yeah, yeah. Sorry, I was in deep thought."

"Thinking about the new shopping center, hey Doc?"

"Yes, it's going to be a great addition to our little town."

"You bet it is, if it doesn't have a big chain grocery store. Otherwise, I'll be out of business."

"People won't leave your fine store and great service," Doc assured him.

"Yeah, wish I could be so confident of that."

Doc drove on home. He needed to prepare dinner before his granddaughter got home from school. They planned an early dinner, so they both could attend the baseball game. How many more games would they attend together? He wondered.

*****

A week passed, and all was normal in Sonderville. The quiet, sleepy town seemed to never change. But the shopping center was still on track to be built in the near future. The boys' baseball team lost the bid for state. Doc had walked downtown to the diner for lunch. It was not an unusual day.

The clouds were gathering as he left the diner. He

said to himself, "I'll go inside the courthouse; the third-floor windows look out onto the plains. I'll go see where the clouds are heaviest."

This was a normal thing for Doc to do. Lots of townspeople climbed those golden oak stairs to the top of the building, just to look out from time to time. People would always see tornadoes dancing on the plains up to fifty miles away. It was the talk of the town during the Spring season.

Today was no different. As he made his way to the top, little Danny Hogg came bolting down the stairs. "Hey, Danny. What did you see up there?" Doc asked.

"It's a twister, mister!"

"Where are you going?"

"To tell my mom! We better get in the storm shelter."

"You, be safe, Danny." Doc said as the little boy ran away.

Doc thought I'd better take a good look at this one. Surely, Danny has seen other twisters, but he was very concerned. Doc had seen as many as a dozen at a time. They did their little dance and stirred up dirt, but then they'd go back up into the clouds and disappear. As long as they were not headed for town, most people ignored them. It was fun to watch them though from the third story window of the courthouse.

Doc stepped up to the window. My, the clouds were thick, dark and heavy. It lessened the distance of the view. He could see several small tornadoes to the west. The one twister, to the south, was the one that scared Danny Hogg. It was by itself and it looked different from the others. It was closer and coming toward Sonderville. This one was wide, and it was threatening.

Doc picked up the binoculars that were always left on the windowsill for people. He surveyed the entire area. The view from on high surveyed a hundred miles of flat land unobstructed by hills or trees. He tried to estimate the distance of the big twister from town.

If it were headed to Sonderville, Doc would need to tell people downtown. They would sound the alarm, a huge siren to let people know to take cover. Doc liked to take cover with some of his friends in the big vault the title company used. Today, however, his granddaughter was getting out of school early and would be home alone. He thought he had best head home.

When he drove up in the driveway, he heard the siren in town blast away. The siren was louder and lasted longer than usual. His granddaughter heard his car and ran outside.

"Gramps, we need to get into the basement."

He left his briefcase in the car and went inside with his granddaughter. They descended the stairs into the basement.

"I wish I had finished this basement out," Doc said.

"It's fine. Come sit here next to me," his

granddaughter said.

He sat down on the couch next to her and put his arm around her to comfort her. Within minutes, the siren sounded again. They both knew the twister was coming into town. They both hoped and prayed quietly to themselves that the twister would jump back up into the clouds.

Living in tornado alley, a person experiences such events many times during their lifetimes. It is only occasionally a twister comes to town. Today was the day.

The swirling wind was fierce. The debris was hitting the house. They could hear the siding being ripped from the walls. Their roof leaving was one big swoosh. The roar of the train sound was deafening. The lights went out and the two held onto each other for life.

Their hearts pounded for fear. Huddling together in the dark was all they could do, and then the silence. Total darkness and silence. Moments passed into minutes and minutes into an hour. They could not move for fear. Then, Doc said, "Come on. It's gone. Let's go see what it did."

They climbed the stairs holding onto the wall because it was so dark. They could not see the staircase. The granddaughter said, "I'm sorry. I should have brought a flashlight." She began to cry.

"Oh, honey. Don't cry. It'll be alright."

Doc turned the knob and pushed the door, but it did not move. He could not open the door. The debris from the demolished house was holding the door shut.

"Let me help," the granddaughter said. They both pushed and pushed, but to no avail. The door did not budge.

Scary thoughts ran through their minds, but they did not want to voice their thoughts and scare the other person. But they both knew they needed help or the basement would become their coffin.

The town suffered immense damage that memorable day. Sonderville was gone. Every house and every business was destroyed or damaged. The hospital was the only area that was untouched. People were arriving at the emergency room by the dozens. There were many injuries and several had succumbed. Where was Doc? All the nurses wanted to know where Doc Salvia was.

It was not like him not to be there quickly after any emergency. People were asking if anyone had seen him or heard from him. When the sheriff got word Doc was missing, he sent a patrol car to his house to check on him.

As the patrol arrived, he called in that Doc's house was gone. The house was totally destroyed on the ground in a heap of rubble. The sheriff had been friends with Doc for many years and the news hit hard. Doc was gone.

The nurses at the hospital heard the news, too. Everyone was sorrowful but scrambling to help patients without Doc's help. Sally, the chief of staff and a long-time friend, asked if anyone had checked the basement of Doc's house. Nobody seemed to know there was a basement.

Immediately, the word went out, and the sheriff sent a crew of men to dig out an area where Sally said there was a basement. Doc and his granddaughter could hear the work and called out. They kept yelling, but the crew could not hear them. It took several hours to get to the bottom of the debris and remove the last timbers from on top of the basement area.

A crewman said he thought he heard noise and the other men began to move things faster. "Surely," one said, "I hear voices."

A few minutes later, Doc and his granddaughter were pulled from the rubble. They hugged every person there that helped to free them. They were uninjured except for the terrifying moments they lived through. It would take time to recover from the mental anguish they both suffered.

The granddaughter held her grandfather and told him, "We will never be separated. Some things are more important than money. I never want to lose you."

Doc smiled, holding her tight and said, "We will be together, wherever it is."

She smiled and nodded. They knew they would find a new home together, whether staying in Sonderville or moving to the big city. It no longer mattered. Location was not as important today as it was yesterday.

The Warning Siren

It was Halloween night in 2023, and I was living in Evanstown when the siren went off. It was loud, and I heard the neighbors yelling at their kids. The night was not yet upon us, as kids were trick-or-treating up and down the street. I could see the Stevens rushing their kids inside, and turning off their porch lights.

The waling of the siren kept pushing out waves of sound like a rushing locomotive. What could be the problem? It was not storming; could it be a tornado alert? There was nothing in the weather report on the evening news about bad weather.

Maybe it was an Amber Alert. We have more and more of those these days. With it being Halloween, nothing would surprise me. The trouble our country and town has seen in the past few years leaves one almost dead to disaster worry.

I closed my door, turned off my porch light, and switched the remote control to see if there was anything on television. My favorite station was black. I clicked to the next, and the next; all the major stations were off. I went to a local station and there was Angela Haybright talking at record speed. I turned up the volume. By now, my heart was racing, wondering what was happening.

The siren was continuing and getting louder. It was ominous. Angela was saying to take cover immediately. Cover? From what was my question? I walked up near the T.V. and listened as she was now yelling to take cover. Prepare for all kinds of emergencies. She was not sure how long their station would be on the air. She said to get food, medicine, weapons, and to shelter in place.

I didn't know what to do. Should I begin preparing for a disaster I knew nothing about, or stay in front of the television for as long as she was on the air? My feet were frozen to that spot. I stood still, waiting for more information.

She said the station was locked down and the people remaining there would stay as long as they had power. Obviously, it was a power outage. She said the whole eastern half of the country was without power. That explained all the major networks being off the air.

She said there would be widespread looting and killing. Stay inside and protect yourself was her advice. I decided at that moment to walk to the bedroom and retrieve my shotgun. Nobody would be breaking into my house without suffering some consequences. Then I remembered I was very low on ammunition. The government had made sure ordinary people could not buy ammunition for the past several years.

I wondered, was this all planned? How long was this in the planning, and was it our government doing it to us, or was there a foreign enemy to blame? It did not matter, if someone tries to break in, I will take care of them myself.

I was determined to protect myself. I reached for my phone to see if it was working. No signal. Hmm, I wondered why? What happened to the electrical grid?

Was it hit? Was it a cyber-attack? I had so many questions, but no answers. The only thing I knew was I had no phone, and only one local station reporting. That ear-busting siren was getting on my nerves.

Looking out the front window, I could see every house in the neighborhood shutdown except for a few lights. No cars were moving and nobody on the street on a Halloween night. What a perfect night to do something like this, I thought. The devil's night and he was going to make the most of it. What kind of evil has brought this upon an unsuspecting population?

Then I remembered how many times we have been warned that something of this magnitude could happen. I was thankful I still had electricity, but how long would it last? I went to the pantry and started laying out all the candles I could find on the counter. There was a lighter and a box of matches. I better draw up some water too, I thought.

How I wished I had prepared better. Now, it was too late. I ran to the bathroom, put the stopper in the tub, and began filling it with water. My car, I thought, needs to be in the garage. I must move it. I turned off the water until I could move my car.

Where are the keys? Oh, yes. Here they are. I lifted the garage door and walked outside. Looking down the street, there was no activity. It looked like a ghost town. The siren was no longer blasting away. I unlocked the car door and got in. I tried to start the car, but there was silence. The motor would not turn over. There were no warning lights on the dash. I knew my car was dead. Was it the battery or had there been an EMP strike?

I locked the car, went back inside, shutting the garage door by hand and went to the television. It was dark inside my home, and the television was dead, too. I had to assume it was an EMP strike and if it was, there would be no restoring electricity for another year or two. Could I survive that long?

All my electricity was off. I lit some of the candles on my kitchen counter. My mind immediately thought about the refrigerator. What can I do to save my food? I had a small generator in the garage, so I went to find it. I had not used it in years. Would it even start, and did I have gas for it? My mind made me even jumpier than the circumstances.

There it was, it didn't look too bad. I opened the gas

tank, and there was gas in it, but it had been in it for at least two years. What was I thinking, not taking care of something as important as a generator? I tried to start it. It would not turn over. There was nothing. I knew then it was fried, and I was in trouble.

My refrigerator food would not last long. The freezer was full of meat, but how could I cook it? I had a Coleman cook stove. Yes, I would cook it that way since my electric range was not going to work. If I cook the meat, it will last a little longer.

I decided to make room in the garage for the camp stove and set up a fold-up table to cook on. Dangerous fumes could stay in the garage, not in the house. I took a large pot from the cupboard and dumped some stew meat in it, and took a couple of steaks and cut them up. I thought it would be easier to cook this way. I put the pot under the faucet to add some water, but there was no water.

Water? No water? What am I going to do?

I ran to the bathroom, turned the faucet on the tub and only a trickle came out. Don't panic, I told myself. I am good in situations like this, I will figure out something.

There was a gallon jug of water in the pantry, so I used that to start cooking my first pot of meat. I added some spices and stood there stirring the meat until my mind considered all the events of the evening.

If I remain calm, I can figure things out better, I kept telling myself. How long before people are starving, and how much danger am I in? The thoughts kept coming to my head. I could not stop the rush of negative thinking.

Stop and evaluate without emotions. Water, food, shelter, safety are all things we are taught. Which order is the best?

I was analyzing the situation and looking for the best solutions. It must be safety first, so that means protecting myself, and that means weapons. I must gather anything I can use as a weapon. Just the thought of using a weapon against a neighbor or anyone brought terror to my heart.

Second is shelter. I have good shelter here at my home. Fortunate enough to live in an area with a mild climate. I won't freeze to death in winter, and I won't burn up in the summer. It may be uncomfortable without utilities, but I can survive.

Third, is water. I have a few bottles of water in my pantry and an inch or two of water in my bathtub. Oh yes, the toilets have water in the tanks. This is not a lot of water, but it will last me for a few days. I must go out and find a source of water. Maybe there is a creek or pond nearby that I can gather some water. I have some bleach to sterilize it, and I can boil it on my camp stove.

Food is the fourth, and I have plenty in my fridge, if it does not all spoil. I wonder what I could do to preserve it? I wish I had thought about this a long time ago and had done something about it. If only I had not procrastinated.

The worry was consuming me. A feeling of desperation overshadowed my whole being. I kept cooking the meat, but what would I do with all of it after it was cooked? I had no refrigeration. Could I eat it all before it spoiled and then what would I eat? The desperation was real, and I knew there were no easy answers. Were my neighbors questioning the same things?

The garage was hot, and the sweat was pouring off my face. I looked at my shirt and it was soaking wet. My head hurt, and then I blacked out.

When I awakened, I was lying on the sidewalk in my front yard. My clothes were wet, my head hurt so badly. Mr. Johns was standing over me saying, "Are you okay?" Mrs. Johns was wiping my face with a cloth.

"What happened?" I asked.

"A hailstorm. You were hit on the head by a huge hail stone," Mr. Johns replied.

"Yes, we were so worried about you. You've been out for several minutes," Mrs. Johns said.

"We called 9-1-1," Mr. Johns added.

"We saw it when it happened," the Mrs. exclaimed. "The ambulance will be here shortly."

The paramedics arrived and checked me out. I was

alright except for the knot on my head which still smarts. It was all a dream, a very bad dream. Actually, it was a nightmare I will never forget. I am thankful I have more time to prepare. Now, I will prepare and not be caught off guard if it should really happen.

Dreams can be signs. I have never put much faith in dreams. But when God smacks you on the head like this, it is a dream worth giving all your attention.

Samuel and the Saucer

Owning and operating Roy's hardware store in my small town has been interesting and fun for the past twenty years. I've come to know most of the residents of Forneyville. My employees have been stable and reliable, except for a few in years past. For the most part, buying this store was a good decision and a great investment. I'm so glad I listened to my wife back then. Everyone needs hardware from time to time.

Samuel came to work for me in 1999. He lost his delivery job when the company almost went broke and laid off people. I didn't know if he'd like this kind of work, but he learned to meet the people and worked steady. He became one of my best employees. He worked hard, was dependable, and never made too many complaints. We got along real fine.

Marilee, the newspaper reporter, kept asking questions about our friendship, me and Samuel, that is. Sure, we were friends at work, but we never really socialized outside of work. I have always kept management and hired help separated. It works best that way.

"Marilee, I told you we never spent time together outside of work. Samuel would go home every evening and kind of kept to himself, as far as I know."

"Roy, did you ever have dinner together or just go to a party or a ball game with Samuel?"

"Marilee, it's like I told you already. He kept to himself. He didn't care for sports and I am not sure if he had any relatives close by. His wife died years ago, and he just made work the center of his life."

"Well, thank you Roy. I appreciate all the information you gave me, and if you think of anything else, just let me know. The sheriff is concerned, and nobody has seen him in two weeks."

"It's the strangest thing. Samuel disappearing like that. Why, I'd almost say those aliens came back and got him."

"Aliens? What aliens?"

"We used to laugh at Samuel behind his back. He thought aliens were out to get him."

Marilee raised her eyebrows and put her pencil on her pad. She was ready to hear this story. I had piqued her interest.

"Well, about six months ago, Samuel came to work one morning. He was all shaken up. He wanted everyone to hear his story. Samuel had gone somewhere, shopping or something, but he got home late. You see, Samuel lived way out in the country."

"Yes, I know. I've been to his house. The sheriff has been out there several times trying to find him."

"It's awful that we don't know where he is. He just up and disappeared."

"That's why the sheriff sent me over here to talk to you."

"I told the sheriff already everything I'm about to tell you."

"I'm sorry for interrupting. Please go on." Marilee leaned forward, not to miss a word Roy was about to tell her.

"Well, Samuel, got all of us gathered together to tell us what happened. He has that big gate at the front of his property. He keeps it locked when he is not there. As he was driving up to his property, he slowed down. He was almost at the gate when he saw a huge saucer come down out of the sky. It hovered just above the ground to the south of his property line, which is right near the gate that leads to his house."

"A saucer? Like a flying saucer, you mean?"

"Yes, a huge flying saucer. He described it as round but kind of flat with flashing lights of different colors circling the sphere."

"And then what happened?"

"Well, he didn't know what to do. It was just sitting there above the ground with the lights flashing. He waited for a few minutes and then decided to get out of his car and unlock the gate."

"I imagine he was plenty scared," Marilee said.

"If it really happened, I would be scared."

"So, you don't think it happened?"

"Oh, come on, Marilee. Do you think it did?

"Well, I don't know. Samuel has disappeared. Anyway, go ahead and finish the story."

Marilee began to write again. "Samuel said, he got out, unlocked the gate, pulled his car through, and then shut and locked the gate again, as usual. He kept his eyes on the saucer, and it continued to float above the ground. It made a slight humming noise, was all. Then Samuel drove to his house. When he got inside, he kept the lights off so he could see down the road. He thought the saucer might follow him home."

Marilee was breathing heavily now. "So, did it follow him?"

"No, he looked out the windows for a couple of hours. The saucer did not move. Finally, he saw the flashing lights rise from the ground, go high into the sky and disappear. Samuel was afraid they would come back and take him for a ride on the saucer. He said he stayed awake all night long, worrying. Now he is missing, so maybe they did come back. We don't know, but we are not making fun of him anymore."

Marilee said, "The sheriff is very concerned. They took cadaver dogs out to search for him, but they came up with nothing."

"Marilee, was the gate locked when the sheriff first went out?" asked Randy, one of Roy's employees.

"Yes, it was. His car is in the garage too. Nobody has seen him or anyone else come and go from his place in two weeks. That's why I'm out here trying to discover anything the sheriff might have missed."

"Well, I told the sheriff about the saucer," Roy added. "My employees were interviewed too, and the sheriff didn't seem too interested in the saucer story."

Marilee motioned for me to walk away from my employees' curious eyes and ears. We walked back into my office.

"Shut the door, Roy. I don't want anyone to hear what I am about to tell you."

I immediately shut the door and was all ears. She sat down, and I also grabbed a seat.

"The sheriff knows more than he is letting on. I have been working on a story for weeks. It seems that Samuel is not the only person in this county that has reported seeing the saucer. Mrs. Landry out on Turkey Creek Road saw it twice last month. She was all upset. She said it came the last time and hovered right above her hen house and scared her chickens so bad they have not laid an egg since."

"You don't say?"

"And that's not all, Roy. Remember the old abandoned cotton gin on Three Springs Road?"

"Yeah, what about it?"

"That structure was old, but it was built to withstand the biggest tornadoes. It no longer is standing. Completely down to the ground. In fact, the bricks are turned into powder."

"What? When did this happen? I was just out that way last week."

"It was discovered two days ago by Bobby Sawyer as he was driving. That's why I am following up on Samuel. I didn't know he saw the saucer, though. The sheriff didn't tell me that. He just said I needed to talk to you."

"I see. So, you think this saucer thing is real?"

"With the new information, I have just now told you about, what do you think?"

"Well, I think we might need to go talk to Mrs. Landry and see what else she can tell us."

"Roy, that is a great idea. Get your coat and let's go."

The drive to Mrs. Landry's didn't take long, but Marilee and I speculated on what else could be the cause of these mysterious happenings. I respected her. She had been a newspaper reporter for at least fifteen years. Her judgment had always been good. She was level-headed,

I would say. She never exaggerated, so I believed what she said.

When we arrived, Mrs. Landry was outside, hanging clothes to dry in the wind. It was a little chilly, but I suppose she was used to it. I beeped my horn, and she turned to see us. Waving, she motioned for us to come up the porch steps. She went inside by the back door and came to meet us at the front door. She welcomed us in.

"Good to see you, but what are you doing here?" Mrs. Landry asked.

Marilee started the conversation and asked her to tell me about the two sightings she had encountered with the saucer. Mrs. Landry loved telling stories, and she went on and on about how the saucer came flying by the first time and then stopped in midair. It hovered above her house for a few minutes and then took off so fast she barely saw it leave.

The second sighting was scarier though, because it just sat above the hen house for about ten minutes or more. Mrs. Landry went outside and walked under the saucer. She said she saw a circular door underneath it. She was afraid it might open at any moment, but she was determined to stand there and watch what would happen. Mrs. Landry said there was a slight humming noise, but not very loud. But this time when it left, it left slowly, and the humming became louder, the higher in the sky it went.

The strangest thing Mrs. Landry told us was the wind all around the saucer was so strong it blew her hair and her dress. She held her dress down from the wind the saucer produced. However, when she stood directly under the saucer, there was no wind. It was completely calm. She could see the dust blowing all around the saucer, but underneath, the ground was still and calm. She said it was eerie.

Mrs. Landry liked to talk, but she was not a lady who would make up things. She was telling us the truth. Her hens had not laid an egg since it happened and she was concerned about that.

"Mrs. Landry, would you mind if we looked at your hens and their nests?" I asked.

"No, not at all. I was thinking about calling the vet."

We all walked outside toward the henhouse. The wind had picked up and dust was blowing. Marilee stood outside the pen and I went inside. Chickens were walking all around me. I suppose they thought I was coming to feed them. I opened the door to the hutch and went inside. The light was on, and I could see their nests quite well.

I gasped! I called to Marilee and Mrs. Landry to come here. "Look!" I said as I pointed to the nests.

The nests were full, overflowing with eggs. Could Mrs. Landry have missed those eggs? Was she telling us the truth?

Mrs. Landry put her hand over her mouth. Her eyes bulged, so did Marilee's.

Marilee said, "How do you explain these?"

Mrs. Landry was shaking her head in disbelief. "I don't know. Those eggs were not there this morning when I came out to feed the chickens."

Marilee suggested we get a basket to gather them. Mrs. Landry stepped outside the hutch to get a basket. And that is when we heard the humming noise. The saucer was overhead.

Mrs. Landry was almost in a trance, it seemed. She dropped the basket and walked outside the pen. She walked beneath the saucer. Marilee and I watched her as she approached the saucer. Mrs. Landry was looking up. The circular door moved to the side, revealing a large open area.

I called to her to stop, not to get any closer. Mrs. Landry never took her eyes off the saucer door. She stood directly under it and her body began to rise off the ground. When she reached the door, she was pulled inside by the same force that lifted her from the ground. The door slowly closed. In a matter of seconds, the saucer flew away, and the wind stopped.

I fell to my knees. I was shaken. Marilee had her mouth open, but she was not saying anything. It took us a few minutes to gain our composure and begin to converse what just happened.

"Did you see what I saw?" she asked.

"I think so. What did you see?"

"In the window, with the blue light?"

"I saw many colored lights in the various windows."

"No, just the blue window."

"I didn't really look at any window in particular. I was just watching Mrs. Landry drift up and go inside."

"In the blue window, I saw the pilot of the saucer."

"You did? Was it a skinny Martian with a big head with big eyes, and no mouth? Like in the movies? What did it look like?"

"No. It looked exactly like Samuel."

"What? Like Samuel? Are you kidding?"

"I'm telling you what I saw. It looked exactly like Samuel. And I could swear he was waving at me. I just stood there, dumbfounded. I didn't even wave back. I was in shock."

"Are we going to call the Sheriff and tell him what we saw? He is not going to believe us."

"I know, but we saw Mrs. Landry go up, and they flew away with her. That's what happened to Samuel, too. Don't you think so?"

"I'll get the Sheriff on the phone and have him come out here."

As I was punching in the phone number, the saucer came back. It stopped above our heads. Marilee and I grabbed hold of one another. We were so frightened. The door underneath opened. Our bodies were pulled from the ground, and inside we went, and the door was closed.

Samuel was standing over me and calling my name. His hands were on my shoulders and he was shaking me. "Wake up, Roy! Lunchtime is over. Time to get back to work."

I wiped my eyes. Apparently, the turkey sandwich I had for lunch had put me to sleep. "I had the craziest dream," I told Samuel. "It was out of this world!"

"Oh, yeah? Was I in your dream?" Samuel said snickering.

"Oh, yeah, buddy. You were definitely in it. I'll tell you about it someday, but not now. We've got work to do."

The Flea Market Gang

As the old jalopy rolled into town, the traffic light turned
red. It was at the corner of Ball Street and Grand Avenue
as Judd and Ethyl sat waiting for the light to change.
Two men dressed in black with hoodies came backing
out of the corner store with guns flashing. The sound of
gunfire erupted in several bursts.

Judd and Ethyl wanted to drive through the red light,
but there was side street traffic. They had to sit still as
the gunmen ran in front of their car, cursing and carrying
canvas bags. Judd and Ethyl sat still, paralyzed, not
knowing what to do.

The gunmen never looked their way as the owner of
the store came running after them with gun in hand. It
was a shootout right before their eyes. Several loud pops
happened before Judd and Ethyl hit the floor of their car.

When things were quiet for a few seconds, Judd
slowly lifted his head. Police sirens were heard in the
background. Surely, the incident had been called in. The
owner of the store stood in front with a crowd of people
talking about what had just occurred.

Police cars were coming from behind and Judd said
to Ethyl, "Let's get out of here." He drove through the

traffic light, which was now green. Ethyl slowly got up and into her seat. She adjusted her hat, which lost its place on her head during the commotion.

"Judd, that was close. Those gunmen could have jumped into our car and we could have been kidnapped."

"Ethyl, don't worry about stuff like that. The good Lord is taking care of us. Those hoodlums didn't even look at us, but I saw them."

"Me too, Judd. I got a good look at them guys."

"Well, maybe we should have stayed and talked to the police, but I just did not want to get involved."

"I know what you mean, Judd. I feel the same way. We could identify those guys and they might come after us after they get out of jail."

"Yep. That's true. Good thing is, those canvas bags looked empty. I think that store owner was on his toes, and he had a gun, too."

"You're right. He kept his store from being robbed because it was a fair fight with both him and them having guns."

"Good thing for him, too. He could have been killed."

"Judd, we could have been killed. They ran right in front of us."

Judd patted Ethyl on the shoulder. "Now, don't worry your pretty little head about this. We are fine. Nothing is going to happen to us. You know the good Lord watches over us."

"I'm not worried. I just want to get to the flea market and get those jelly jars that woman is advertising for half price."

"We're almost there. See, there is the turn just ahead."

The flea market had expanded, and it covered many acres on the outskirts of town. There were vendors from all over the state that kept booths open every weekend. The products sold there ranged from furniture to homemade crafts, to décor of every kind, to food products and beauty care.

Judd and Ethyl came at least once a month to the flea market. They were well acquainted with some of the vendors. Ethyl made it a practice of never skipping on the funnel cakes and had become friendly with the lady that ran the concession stand. Mary was her name, and she gave a friendly wave each time she saw Ethyl walking down the lane where her stand was located.

"Judd, first things first."

"I know. You've got to have your funnel cake. Here's a few dollars. Get me one too."

Ethyl came to the window, holding up two fingers. Mary smiled and nodded. She made Ethyl's first by swirling the batter into the hot oil. When it was golden brown, she flipped it gently. Removing it from the oil, she drained it on paper towels and then sprinkled it with confectioner's sugar. For Ethyl, she added some melted white chocolate in wide circles. She sprayed whipped cream on and topped it with a maraschino cherry.

Ethyl said, "Mary, you're an angel."

Mary smiled and made Judd's funnel cake without the extras. He got the confectioner's sugar, but not the other toppings. He didn't care. Knowing Ethyl and Mary were enjoying a little girl's gag on him.

Mary and Ethyl talked while Judd enjoyed his sweet treat sitting at one of the four picnic tables in front of Mary's stand. After finishing eating, he left the girls while they were talking to go to the next booth to look at some power tools. Ethyl eventually joined him. She was still licking her fingers when she found him checking out a new drill.

"What do you need that for? You've got six of them already."

"You never know when one might go out. Mine are getting pretty old."

"Oh, come on! Let's go look at the metal art."

"Metal art? What's that? I thought we came for jelly jars?"

"You know, when they take an old hand saw or some other hand tool and paint a picture on it. Kathy has two of those painted saws in her living room now, and I was thinking one might look good in our living room."

"Ethyl, you come up with some crazy ideas. But if you want one, we'll get it."

"Judd, wait until you see them. Kathy has one with an old house painted on it, with a tractor sitting out in front. It's really pretty, but I like her other one the best. It has an old man fishing on the creek bank with the sun going down. The colors are vibrant, and I want one just like it. It reminds me of you, sweetheart."

"Okay, Ethyl. I've already said we can get whatever you want. You're the decorator."

Ethyl smiled and looped her arm around Judd's arm as they strolled leisurely down the lane, looking at the various vendor booths. The metal art was at the end of the lane, so they stopped at each booth before getting there.

"Look, Judd. Here are some fancy diamond rings, and they are reasonably priced. I could use a ruby ring or an emerald ring. They have lots of jewelry. And look, what bargains!"

Judd pulled Ethyl away from the booth. "You don't need anything in there."

"But Judd," she protested.

"I said come on, and let's go to the metal art booth." Judd held Ethyl's arm tightly and walked quickly away.

"What's wrong with you? You've never treated me like this? What's going on? Are you wanting to see one of those painted saws now?"

Judd ignored the question and kept walking with his gaze in front of himself. He pulled on Ethyl's arm. When they were three booths away, Ethyl stopped and said, "What's wrong with you? Talk to me."

"Will you keep on walking? I'll tell you when we get to the metal art booth."

Ethyl walked along with a scowl on her face. When they got only a little distance from the booth, Judd whispered in her ear. Ethyl's eyebrows lifted and her eyes got big. She swallowed hard and said, "I'm sorry. No wonder you were acting so strange."

Judd recognized the two men sitting in the back of the booth as the two men that ran in front of their car earlier. Of course, they were selling jewelry. They had just tried to rob a jewelry store.

Ethyl said, "That explains the bargain prices. Those rings were real, weren't they? I didn't know for sure when I was looking. I couldn't understand how they could sell expensive jewelry for the low prices that were marked."

"Yes, and at a flea market. Nobody would think they were real. They probably make a good amount selling stolen merchandise. I wonder how long they have been out here?"

"We've got to call the police, Judd."

"I've got a better idea. You know Mary's brother is a policeman and does security out here at the flea market.

Suppose we just tell him and go home. We will let the police do their thing. He will need to call for backup."

"That's a good idea. Once they arrest them, they will find out about all their merchandise. It sure is brazen of them to be out here selling when they just tried to rob a store in the same town."

"Ethyl, these are hard times. The criminals are more brazen, and the police are fewer. We have to be careful, too. I am just so glad we saw them and can identify them."

"Yes, maybe that will be two criminals off the street. Can we get a metal art before we go?"

"Ethyl! We will come back in a few days and get whatever you want. But not today, okay?"

Ethyl nodded her head in agreement. She and Judd walked to the security office. There, they found Mary's brother and two other officers. They told them what they saw, and they called the local police. Within minutes, all roads in and out of the flea market were closed off with patrol cars. A unit of officers surrounded the booth where the supposed robbers were. Judd and Ethyl were right. It was the same men.

After their arrest, the police recovered merchandise from numerous robberies that had occurred in the past two years, in a radius of a hundred miles from the flea market. Two other persons were also arrested and charged with theft. The police were ecstatic to have solved so many crimes with this initial arrest.

Judd and Ethyl were interviewed on television. They became celebrities at the flea market. Today, they enjoy free funnel cakes anytime they visit, and there is a painted saw blade above the couch in their living room. It hangs next to a photograph of the two of them, with the police commissioner presenting them with a letter of appreciation and a reward check from Tipsters Anonymous. Below the picture is says, 'Crime doesn't pay, but tips do.'

Rest With Me

There is a place where I love to go. It is high on the mountaintop. The wind blows gently there at all times. It barely rustles the dry grass in winter, but it is always there. Closing my eyes, I can feel it on my cheeks. It whistles a small gust of air now and then, reminding me of its presence.

The view of the mountains is so serene with rounded tops scalloped across the sky. The clear blue is swished with white streaking clouds caused by the ever-present wind. Silence there is so loud it screams and makes my heart faint.

I stand and reach my arms upward in praise to God for His marvelous works. The breeze blows stronger, until my clothes whip about my body. The force of the wind could now knock me to my knees, but it does not need to, as my frame gently bows to the magnificence of the moment.

Holy Spirit, is that you I feel? Is it you coming to spend time with me, or have I come to spend time with you? Peace, joy, and happiness is what I feel, and the desire for more times like these is all-consuming. The breeze relents.

Please, don't leave me. Not now, not ever.

The breeze bursts out a gust that shakes the brown leaves from the oak nearby. The leaves float down to the ground. I pick up the largest one. It is the size of my whole hand. Brown with gold veins and curled on the edges. It says my tree is at rest. Rest with me until winter is over and then dance with me in the Spring.

King James Version
Matthew 11:28-30

28 Come unto me, all ye that labour and are heavy laden, and I will give you rest.

29 Take my yoke upon you, and learn of me; for I am meek and lowly in heart; and ye shall find rest unto your souls.

30 For my yoke is easy, and my burden Is light.

Chapter 7
Men Love to Read Too!

The Wonders of Chili

Chili is a superfood in my family. My dad made the chili in his later years. He loved mixing all the spices after he browned the meat. He cooked the pinto beans for hours before he started the chili making. Dad used canned tomatoes and chopped a large onion. Using fresh garlic and chopped celery added to the unique flavor of my dad's chili.

I watched him, always smiling, as he prepared the tasty stew. It was his hobby to make a big pot of chili once a week and invite the neighbors to come and enjoy. Chili day was a social gathering at my parents' house.

The delectable spices simmering all day long left the warmth in every room. Walking through the front door, everyone knew it was a special day. A big bowl, a spoon and an absorbent napkin were all that was needed. However, with the crackers served, also came hot homemade cornbread and sweet cream butter. But no meal at my parent's home was complete without a bunch of green onions, sliced tomatoes, and fresh radishes from the garden when in season.

My folks believed in feeding hungry people. They enjoyed sharing what they had and invites were never formal. People who knew my parents knew they were always welcome. There was always plenty to go around.

That is their legacy. Hospitality. What a great way to be remembered. Those days are gone, along with my folks, but the chili recipe remains.

I made a big pot today. It was cold outside, and it tasted so good. The spices were just right and it warmed our tummies, but the biggest warmth came to our hearts as we shared with the couple next door. They have very few visitors and often seem lonely. A big bowl of chili opens up conversations that otherwise would never take place. I love chili. This superfood warms everyone.

As we sat around their kitchen table sharing this hot meal, we talked about old times. It seems many years ago, our old neighbor Sam worked with my dad at a factory in town. Sam remembered Joe, and he told us all kinds of stories about my dad I had never heard before. Sam was a youngster when he started working there, and my dad was older and showed him the ropes. They had many lunch breaks together, but never had any of my dad's chili until today.

Isn't it strange what a small world we live in? Knowing Sam and Edith better now, I feel closer to my dad. He would be happy to know his chili is still making the neighbors happy.

Paying It Forward

Standing in line at the register, I saw him reach into his back pocket for his wallet. When he pulled it out in front, I saw his name imprinted there. Flipping it open, he pulled out a credit card.

"Here," he said, as he handed me the card. "I want to pay for those people at table number four." He pointed in the direction of the table as the waitress was removing the dishes from their table.

"Alright, let me get their ticket," I said. I walked to the waitress, and she gave me a ticket. Coming back, I rang up his first, and then added theirs to his bill. Handing him the receipt, he started to walk away.

The couple at the table realized what he had done. The man yelled to him to stop and come over. Jim turned to them, smiled and walked to their table.

The man said, "Why did you just pay for our meal?"

Jim replied, "You are a veteran, are you not, sir?"

"I am. How did you know?"

"It's written on your ball cap, Vietnam Veteran. How else can I say thank you, but by buying a meal?"

"Well, thank you, young man!"

"The name's Jim. Jim Ryder. And yours?"

"I'm Timothy Warner, and this is my wife, Jeannine."

"Pleased to meet you both."

"We are pleased to meet you, Jim. Won't you have a seat and visit for a while?"

"Yes, I'd like that."

The waitress brought them fresh glasses of water while they talked non-stop. I couldn't help but hear the conversation with the register being located nearby.

The late morning conversation turned into hours of long talking. The breakfast crowd left, and the lunch crowd arrived before Jim and his new friends finished their visit. They had so much to talk about. Jim was interested in Timothy's Vietnam tours and had many questions. The old veteran was eager to share his memories.

"My first tour in Vietnam began in 1965," Timothy shared. "I was stationed at Nha Trang and my job was on C-123's. We started with B models and later, two J85 jets were added and they became K models."

"Please go on, but tell me first, did you know or ever meet Tom Ryder? He was my father. He was there about that time, but he never made it back. Not sure if it was Nha Trang? My mother would know, but she is gone now. I have some old photographs, but I need to get them out and look at them again. Maybe we can look at them together sometime."

"We lost some mighty good guys in that war. Like every war, good people die. I am so sorry for your loss,

Jim."

Jeannine said, "Yes, we are sorry for your loss. I am sure your dad was a great man. He served his country, and you should be very proud of him."

"I am, Jeannine. My dad was my hero. They don't make them like that anymore." He sighed, and there was silence for a moment. "You know, he gave his life, saving a Vietnamese woman and her baby. She was walking down the street and a Viet Cong company in a truck was heading right at her. My dad ran in front of her, pulling her away, but got hit by the truck. The truck plowed into a building and exploded. My dad died from the explosion because he was injured and could not get out of the way after the truck hit him."

"He saved the woman, though?" Jeannine asked.

"Yes, she was very grateful, and she and my mother wrote letters back and forth for years."

"Really? That is selflessness," Timothy said.

"Yes, my dad was a caring person. He cared about everyone. He hated war, but was loyal to his country and served with pride."

"I wish I could have known him. He certainly raised a good son."

"Thank you. I try to make my dad proud. Meeting veterans and expressing gratitude to them is my little way of paying it forward."

"Well, you didn't have to pay for our meal, but we

are thankful you did. The biggest thanks are that you let us know your appreciation. When we came back from Vietnam, we did not get a hearty welcome. It was a stain on our country. So, the change in attitude the country has taken is appreciated."

"Of course, I have always appreciated the veterans since my dad died over there. Tell me more about what happened to you, Timothy."

"Well, like I said, I was stationed at Nha Trang on the first tour of duty. Then, in 1971, I was stationed at Phan Rang. I flew airplanes. We sprayed Agent Orange to kill the foliage and malathion to kill the insects. You know how many people got sick from that poison. We had to be in the sky at first light. It could not be over 85 degrees when we sprayed, so it happened at dawn. We flew barely above the treetops and often took fire.

We moved troops and gear. We picked up injured soldiers and flew planes back and forth. We went where we were needed and did what needed to be done. That's about all I can say about it. It wasn't easy, and I thank God I lived to tell the story."

Jeannine put her hand on Timothy's, and tears welled up in her eyes as she remembered the past. Jim saw her reaction and turned his attention to her.

"I imagine it was a hard time for you, as well, Jeannine. I know it was for my mother. She talked about it enough for me to know the pain she felt, and the loneliness from losing my dad."

Timothy told about different incidences that happened on missions flying into the jungles of Vietnam and Laos and Cambodia. There were constant missions; the planes were in the sky day and night. Timothy barely had time to sleep, and could eat a sandwich in a few bites while running from one mission to another.

He said he was constantly on an adrenaline high, staying alert for danger from all sides. When he was in the air, there were shots being fired at the planes. When he was on the ground, there was the possibility of explosions and armed attacks. Danger was always present, and being on alert wore the body and mind down. Many lost everything in the war.

Timothy shared that Patches, a C-123 airplane, was one of the planes he flew. Patches is now in the Air Force Museum in Dayton, Ohio. There are bullet holes still visible in the planes' skin. Timothy remembers when those shots hit.

The thinking that killed morale in the armed forces were the protests at home. Not having support from the American people, especially the youth, was more than hurtful. It caused many suicides, and the lingering effects took lots of lives even after the war was over.

Jim listened intently. He knew Timothy was still recovering from the pain of the war. He thought his dad would have felt the same way if he had lived.

Timothy went on to say that when people like Jim recognize the sacrifices his generation made, it makes a difference. Healing has happened in many Vietnam veterans' lives. But then, he said, "You know what is going on in the streets today is similar to what happened back then. Many young people don't respect our government today like they should, and they don't want to fight for our country. If they refuse, America will fall. Our freedoms will be lost forever."

Jim replied, "That is why I do all I can to bring attention to those who gave for our country and our freedoms. I call it 'Paying It Forward'. I am writing a book about veterans. Timothy, would you allow me to tell your story in my book?"

"What? Me, in a book? Why, I would be so proud. Let me tell you about my friend Jerry. He was shot down two times and survived. We were in the same hospital in Japan recovering when our friendship began. He died last year, but his widow would love for his story to be told, as well. Can we do that?"

"You bet we can! Let's get together in a few days and talk some more. Here is my card with my office address and phone number. Give me a call and we can meet there, and I'll show you what I have in mind for my book."

"Sounds great." Timothy reached out his hand to Jim. That was the first time he realized Timothy's hand was a prosthetic. Obviously, he had lost more in the war than he had told Jim. There would be lots of time to discuss more, and Jim looked forward to those talks.

As Jim rose from the table, Jeannine said, "Do you have a name for your book?"

Jim nodded his head. Smiling, he said, "Yes, it's going to be called Paying It Forward."

The Old Hunter

November comes and the excitement of deer season keeps the old hunter busy preparing his hunting clothes. They've been stored all year waiting for opening day. Long-sleeved camo shirts, camo pants, thermal underwear and his beloved coveralls. A jacket and hat to match with an orange vest is all that is needed to make his attire complete. Just unpacking and trying on is a chore, with his frozen shoulder and bone spurs in the joint of his right shoulder. He works through the pain, because his love of hunting is more important than this suffering he must endure.

In times past, baiting and feeding were accomplished in the weeks prior. Today, there is no baiting because of chronic wasting disease. Trail cams are checked, and times of movement are recorded. He analyzes each animal and estimates its age. The stalking and the watching of the animals is thrilling. Opening day of deer season is coming and all preparations have been made. The thrill is at its height. Hunting conversations have been at the top of the mind and shared with all his friends.

5:00 a.m. comes and the alarm should ring, but the old hunter awakened from excitement a few minutes earlier and turned it off. He rises, and dresses with pain throbbing, as he lifts his arm, putting on the hunting clothes that describe him as deer slayer. Moving quietly to avoid waking his sleeping wife, he makes the coffee and fills his thermos. Checking his pack, bundling up tightly in heavy clothes and coveralls, he goes to the garage to retrieve the 4 by 4.

He ties the gun case down to the bed of the ATV. Moves out quietly from the garage and heads down the trail with only headlights in the dark of the night. Untying the gun case and lifting it from the machine sends acute pain up his arm and into the shoulder and back. He grimaces. A moment later, as the pain subsides, he can now lift the gun onto his left shoulder, and carry the pack up the stairs of the deer blind. With only the flashlight on the brim of his cap, he is careful not to arouse the wildlife of his presence.

Inside the deer stand, he prepares for hunting before the sun rises. Thermos of coffee and propane heater will keep him warm. The night gives way to shadows of dawn. An occasional chirp or tweeting awakens the forest from slumber.

Arthritis pains ache in the old hunter's legs and back,

but it is the frozen shoulder that gives him the most pain. Some days it is unbearable, even with rest and pain relievers. Unable to raise his right arm but a few inches without excruciating pain makes hunting almost impossible. Still, he manages to unpack his gun and place it on the shelf in front of the open window. There will be no bullets placed in the chamber. He is ready though, if he decided he could do it. His hands are steady, his aim sure, and his eyes have not dimmed with age. But shooting a deer would mean dragging and field dressing it. The process runs through his mind. Unable to lift his arm, and without the strength he had as a young man, hunting has taken on a different realm.

The arm and shoulder don't work well enough to allow the production of venison any longer. The old hunter knows his limitations, but he is still determined to go through the motions of hunting. It is in his blood and in his heart, and races in his memories. He will not give in to his pain.

Since he was a child, with bb gun in hand, he has hunted. First looking for birds and squirrels, then to deer, hogs, and elk. A hunter is always a hunter. The thrill of the tracking, the watching, and the waiting are more than the kill. So, the old hunter spends hours watching with binoculars when he can stand the pain of a raised arm, spying with cameras, only to go home empty-handed.

His wife welcomes him back with smiles and asks about all the animals he saw. He explains the morning in great detail with emphasis on each 'what might have been'. She knows the possibilities keep him going.

It is the hunt he loves. The kill can be forgotten now. Maybe a photo or two will help him remember the one that got away. There are still antlers on the wall in his favorite rooms, a reminder of times past.

The old hunter will come in and take a nap, only to go out in the late afternoon once again for the evening hunt. It is a regimen practiced multiple times during the season. Why does he do it? He wants to believe he still can, while reality is not something he wants to think about.

Uncle Harry's Chocolate Fix

When Danny was a young boy, he lived three doors down from Uncle Harry. I am not sure to this day if Uncle Harry was really his uncle. Every kid in the neighborhood called him Uncle Harry. He was a kind man with a soft, pudgy middle that jiggled when he laughed. Laugh, he could do. Uncle Harry was always making jokes, and laughing was contagious when you were in his presence.

Danny was always sitting on Uncle Harry's front porch when I got off the school bus and passed by. I wondered if he went there every day. He probably did. Danny and Uncle Harry seemed inseparable.

There was a small grocery store at the end of the street. They sold groceries on credit back then, and most people in the neighborhood bought all their supplies from Mr. Maynard. He knew what it took to make and keep loyal customers.

Uncle Harry and Danny had a regular routine of

walking down to the store for chocolate candy. Uncle Harry and Danny often had dried dark chocolate in the corners of their mouths. They were two peas in a pod, so to speak. Chocoholics is what we would call them today.

I never saw Uncle Harry with any other color shirt on than brown. I assumed it was to hide any chocolate that fell on his clothes. But then again, maybe he just liked the color brown.

Mr. Maynard watched every day about three in the afternoon for the pair to come through the old wooden screen that hung on the front door of the store. It would slam and Danny would yell out. "Mr. Maynard, we are here for our chocolate fix!"

Mr. Maynard would come from the meat counter or from behind the register, depending on what he was doing at the moment. He would walk to the candy aisle and hold up two chocolate candy bars. "I've got them right here, gentlemen."

Danny would run to his side and reach for the bars. Mr. Maynard would smile, handing him the candy. "Right this way, unless you need something else today."

"Nope, that's it for today." Uncle Harry paid for the candy in coins. He always had a pocket full of coins that jingled when he walked. I suppose he liked the sound of money jangling in his pocket. People would notice, and maybe he liked that.

The daily ritual played out for years. I was a little

jealous. I had nobody to take me to the store and buy candy for me every day. However, there were times when I passed by Uncle Harry's house that he would call out to me. "Hey, come up here."

He would hand me a candy bar, and pat me on the head and say, I deserved it with all the walking I was doing coming and going to the school bus stop. Uncle Harry was an observant man, and I am sure he gave away more candy than he ever ate. My other friends have fond memories of Uncle Harry, and I know they must be memories like mine.

Uncle Harry died many years ago, but children never forget the kindness adults show to them. Chocoholics was not a term we used back in the day, but there are many chocoholics living today that came from that neighborhood.

Winter Joy

Pretty little round birds,
Come to my porch
Looking for seeds
I scatter and leave.

The snow is cold and deep,
Hides the food from sight.
Porch table is perfect place
Because it's high and dry.

I watch secretly,
From my window quietly.
Little birds will never know,
How much I love them so.

What joy their presence brings,
Whenever I hear them sing.
Little creatures come and dine,
The pleasure is all mine.

Chapter 8   God Laughs

KJV

Genesis 21:6 - And Sarah said, God hath made me to laugh, so that all that hear will laugh with me.

God Laughs

As Maribeth passed by the supervisor's office door, aware of the seething hatred the supervisor had for her, she hurried to her cubicle to correct the paper files. Judith had told Maribeth the files were needed by noon. The supervisor had a meeting to attend, and the files would be going with her.

Maribeth did her best to make her supervisor happy. No matter what she did, how accurate she was with her work, the supervisor never smiled or said thank you. She would begrudgingly grab the papers from Maribeth's hand. Turn in a huff, and march away. Maribeth felt the rejection, but prayed for her supervisor's attitude to change toward her and the other employees. The more she prayed, the worse the situation became.

The tension in the building was so strong everyone could feel it from the moment they entered. Nobody talked about it. Job security was at stake. Faces were drawn, shoulders slumped, and dread filled the air.

Maribeth needed the job and could not quit. She asked to be transferred to a different department, but the requests fell on deaf ears. She knew the supervisor was taunting her at every angle to force her out of her job. Maribeth prayed harder. It became more and more difficult as the days passed.

Maribeth's workload was increased beyond human capabilities, but she endured. It was a test of her strength, but it was the strength of the Lord that invigorated Maribeth. Her supervisor did not realize she was actually fighting against God. Maribeth kept a sweet attitude toward the supervisor and was always kind. The supervisor was not kind to Maribeth. Maribeth would cry out to the Lord at night, but still remained in the job. She was enduring for the sake of the supervisor. She tried many times to talk to the supervisor about various things, but she was never received with the kindness she had shown.

One day, the supervisor was absent. She had a terrible disease. The days went by, and the supervisor was unable to come back to work. Maribeth prayed for her health and for total recovery. Maribeth sent cards and messages, but they were never acknowledged.

Then, the news came that the supervisor did not recover. Her position was now vacant. Maribeth applied for the position and was promoted to supervisor. The office is now running efficiently, and there is a lighter atmosphere. All the employees seem to be happier. There are smiles, and thank you is heard every day within the building.

Psalm 37:12-13
King James Version
12 The wicked plotteth against the just, and gnasheth upon him with his teeth.
13 The Lord shall laugh at him: for he seeth that his day is coming.

The Heart Attack

The sun has been shining brightly all day, but the roads are still covered with snow and ice. Pat and Carol are backing out of their driveway. Nobody else in the neighborhood has ventured out on this sub-zero day. They must have somewhere important to go, or they would stay inside like everyone else. Some days it is just too cold to go out.

Thirty minutes later, they pull into the hospital parking lot. They made it there, even though they had to cross the long bridge over the icy river that leads into town. The sidewalks have been cleared, and there is sand on them to give people a better chance of not falling.

A uniformed officer greets them at the door, and asks them to empty their pockets into a basket on the table. Pat quickly complies and Carol opens her purse and hands it to the officer. Pat grabs his heart once again and moans before he hits the floor. Carol screams.

A nurse standing by the front counter runs to help.

The officer lends a hand too. The nurse turns Pat over on his back and checks his pulse and breathing. A gurney is being wheeled down the corridor as the nurse begins CPR.

Carol is shaking and crying. The doctors and nurses take Pat immediately into the emergency room, and Carol is instructed to wait in the waiting room. She is alone there, except for a couple in the corner, both of whom are coughing. Carol sits on the other side of the room from them.

People pass by and sometimes sit down for a short while. Nobody seems to want to talk. Carol is pacing the floor and constantly asking the receptionist when she can go back to see her husband. The receptionist checks with the emergency room, and they have not given her permission to come back yet.

Carol is beside herself. What if Pat doesn't make it? She tries to not let herself think that way. She is praying and asking for Pat's healing and recovery.

She has called her pastor, and soon he arrives and prays with Carol. It helps to calm her fears, knowing someone is there for her. Then, her best friend from church comes into the waiting room. Betty is looking for her and the pastor. They join their hands and stand in a circle and pray aloud. Nobody seems to care. The prayers are powerful, and all three have tears in their eyes. Betty hugs Carol, and so does the pastor. They sit and wait with her, holding her hands, letting her know they are there for her.

Carol says, "How do people get by without God and without Christian friends? I just don't know how they do it."

The pastor nods his head in agreement. Betty pats Carol's hand and says, "We are blessed to have one another. We are family."

The pastor walks to the receptionist and asks again about Pat's condition and when Carol can go back to see him. The receptionist says, "I just got confirmation he is going to be alright. Carol can go back now."

Carol heard the conversation and jumped up. She turned to Betty and the pastor. "Thank you both for your prayers and support. I needed you so much, and so did Pat. We are thankful for you."

The pastor said, "Don't worry about us. Go on back and see Pat. Tell him we are here and praying. We will be here until you come back out. We're not leaving."

Carol spent the next few hours with Pat, and he was stabilized. The doctors wanted him to spend the night and do more tests tomorrow. Carol told him she would go home and get a bag and come back and stay with him all night. He was happy about that.

The pastor and Betty were waiting for her when she came back from the emergency room. They were happy to hear he was doing well. They told her they would leave and come back tomorrow morning. She thanked them again for their support. "I just don't know what I'd do without my church family."

The pastor offered to walk Carol to her car. Betty said, "We don't know what we'd do without you two. We love you. God bless you."

The couple sitting in the corner still had not been seen by the doctors. There were too many emergencies, and their cases were not considered critical, so they had to wait longer. As Betty was leaving, the lady called to her. "What church do you attend?"

"Calvary Temple on Ridgeway Avenue. Why?"

"We've been watching you and your pastor, and we think we'd like to come visit. We need a church and a church family like you have."

"You are very welcome, and we'd love to have you come. Give me your phone number and I'll give you mine. I'll call and remind you of the service times if you like. I'll meet you at the door and you can sit with me."

"That sounds great. We have to get well first. This coughing has to stop, but when it does, we will be there."

Betty asked if it would be okay to pray for them now. They said yes, of course. Betty held their hands and prayed for their healing.

The pastor had already walked to his car and did not hear the conversation. He was on the phone when Betty walked out. She motioned to him and walked up to his door. He rolled the window down, and she told him what the couple in the waiting room had said.

He was so pleased. "It goes to show you that when you live your testimony in public, people watch. They want what we have. Let's share our Jesus more."

The next day, tests were run on Pat. The tests revealed no damage to the heart, and Pat left the hospital with an appreciation for life. He looked at Carol and said, "God heard and answered your prayers, and that is why I am healthy once again. I know it's true. God heard your prayers, and He is laughing at the amazement the doctors are feeling right now. They can't explain it away. God answers prayer!"

Hollering Holly

Hollering Holly was her name,
Pressures made her not the same.
"Take these pills, and get some rest."
Does the doctor always know what's best?

"It is Stress," the doctor said.
"Go home, and go to bed."
"No, I cannot do that,
I'd go looney as a bat."

I've got work to do all night,
Forms to fill and clients to fight.
Nobody knows the pressure I feel,
Crying out to God, I kneel.

Help me, help me, please.
It's more than I can stand.
Dear God, please reach down,
And give me your helping hand.

I always wanted to be an EA,
Not knowing I'd be to blame,
For any mistakes that were made,
The IRS could come and raid.

What stress and pressure there is,
Nothing is ever totally bliss.
Figures, and figure it out,
Calculate without any doubts.

Nobody told me it would be
Difficult, nothing good to see.
Long days and sleepless nights,
Rest has taken its lonely flight.

Turkey makes you sleepy,
Open eyes, constantly weepy.
Melatonin, please take effect,
My body is in neglect.

John tiptoes to not disturb,
Crankiness is the verb,
He uses to describe his boss,
Without him, I'd be at a loss.

Then it happened around midnight,
Somebody, maybe God, turned out the light.
Sleep, sleep, glorious sleep it came,
How marvelous now, top of my game.

I laughed today, at myself,

My client caused my head to swell.
"What a good job, you've done.
You're the best in the business, Hon."

Things don't always go right,
Even though I try with all my might.
To do the best I can for those,
Who trust me, as one who knows.

So hollering Holly is not my name,
I laughed and joked without shame.
Oh, it feels so good to be,
Happy again, and totally me!

The Prankster

It was the day before April Fool's Day in 1967. Stuart Creepbow was a classmate of mine. I ignored Stuart most of the time. His friends called him Stuie, and his real friends called him Stu. Stuart had many names. Some of those names were said behind his back and others were right to his face.

Stu, Stuie, or Stuart did not care. Nobody could shake his confidence. He was the class clown, and everything was funny to him. The class laughed along with his silly jokes, and as long as someone was laughing, Stu was clowning.

Stu found his way to the principal's office on a regular basis. The teachers had a hard time keeping the class order when Stu was around. He would be told repeatedly to stop clowning, sit in his seat, do his work, and stop disrupting the class. Teachers pulled their hair out, trying to make Stu behave.

Stu was popular at lunchtime. Everyone wanted to sit by him in the lunchroom and walk around with him during breaks. The girls pushed their way near to him, and he loved the attention. The guys hung around Stu also, because that was where the girls were found.

Stu loved to prank people on the telephone. He would call up people he didn't know and ask them if their refrigerator was running. When they said yes, he'd tell them to go catch it from running away. He would laugh and hang up.

This was before caller identification was invented and pranksters could get away with such jokes. I remember one day he called my mom and told her there was something on the roof. She talked to him for several minutes before he said, "Shingles!" He hung up, laughing. My mom was not tickled because she burned something on the stove during the time she was talking to him.

My mom called his mom, and he got in trouble. After that, he followed me around at school, calling me a crybaby. He would bellow and boo behind me as he followed me down the hall, calling me a crybaby. It was my mom that called his mom, not me. Why did he have to pick on me?

Stu was different for sure. It seemed like he never paid the price for his practical jokes, even the ones that went badly. He was super lucky. When he would go to the principal's office, everyone would wait quietly to hear if he got licks. Most of the time, he walked out strutting like a tomcat.

The principal and the secretary would be heard

laughing all the way down the hall. One time, I was getting a drink of water from the water fountain and the principal walked out with Stu. He patted him on the back and was laughing and shaking his head. I thought, 'Some punishment!'

Stu made an impression on everyone he met. My friends, Carol and Brenda, did not care for Stu. We watched his antics from afar. We did not want to be the focus of one of his practical jokes, so we kept our distance.

Poor Dovie Schnell was not so smart. She loved Stu. Dovie was a sweet, but quiet girl. She made good grades and rarely talked in class because she was so shy. We tried to warn her about Stu, but she did not want to hear what we had to say. She said people misunderstood him.

Stu was funny, but often his jokes went too far and someone got hurt. He didn't seem to care as long as he got the praise for his pranks. Embarrassing people was something Stu could do easily.

When he put glue on the door handles, nobody saw him. We all knew who did it. When the toilet paper was missing from the girls' bathroom and it was found in the boys' bathroom, we knew who did it. Volleyball practice was delayed because all the balls were flat. The needles used to air the balls up were missing. We knew who did that.

Stu was one of a kind. His greatest prank was done to

Mrs. Springster. She was the language arts teacher. You did not waste time in her classroom. She taught from the moment you walked in until the bell rang. She gave us lots of homework, and making a good grade in her class was difficult.

Stu did not want to be in her class. She ruled with an iron fist, so to speak. She held him down better than the other teachers. Mrs. Springster was not a pushover. She rarely smiled, and Stu could not get past her determined frown. She was a match he'd never met before. Stu was determined to bring her around before the end of the year. The game was on, even if Stu was the only one playing.

Stu tried to get to her class before she arrived every day. He would move things around on her desk. He used the glue trick again. Stu came in early and put glue on the chalkboard eraser, so when she picked it up, it would be stuck to her hand. He was snickering all morning for that one. But to his surprise, Mrs. Springster changed her daily plan.

She asked for volunteers to come write words on the board. Missy, Charles, and Van wrote words, phrases, and sentences. She was pleased. Then, Mrs. Springster praised them for their work. She said, "Stu doesn't like to take part in class, but today he will enjoy erasing the board for those of us who enjoy learning."

Stu was put on the spot to erase the board with the

eraser that had glue on it. Mrs. Springster turned the tables on him. He took his time, so that the bell rang before he was finished. Everyone left the room before he was trying to remove the eraser from his hand. Everyone except me. I smiled and then burst out in laughter as I left the room. Stu hated me forever for that.

I knew April Fool's Day was coming. Stu would dream up something wild for that day. I asked my mom if I could just stay home from school. I did not want to be the recipient of one of Stu's jokes. My mom declined my request, and I trudged the six blocks to the building.

When I arrived, there was a large crowd gathered around the big oak tree that was opposite the principal's office. Everybody was looking up. I rushed up to see what everyone was looking at. It was a little puppy in a trap cage. The cage was hung on the biggest tree limb and the puppy was whimpering and whining to come down.

Our principal had been summoned. The puppy belonged to the principal and someone had taken the puppy from his house and put it in the cage and slung a rope around the tree limb. The cage was lifted and tied to the tree.

It would have been easily untied and brought down if the rope had not been smeared with honey. Red ants covered the knotted rope. The principal was furious! This joke had gone too far, even for Stu. He would not be getting out of this one.

People started looking for Stu. The principal even called out his name. "Stu, where are you?" He was so angry. No one could find Stu.

"Uh, oh. This means real trouble." I said to Carol and Brenda. "We need to know where Stu is."

"Right." Carol said.

"And what he is up to now?" Brenda agreed.

After searching the hallways, the lunchroom, the bathrooms, the auditorium, we all came up empty. The bell sounded. We needed to get to class. Surprisingly, in every class I had with Stu, he was missing.

I heard later that day; the principal called Stu's mom. She said Stu was sick in bed with the measles. I stopped by his house after school to see for myself. His mom told me he was sick in bed, and I could not come in. "He has the measles."

Something just did not add up. Measles on April Fool's Day? That's it! It's April Fool's Day and Stu has talked his mom into saying he has measles. Tomorrow, she will send an excuse slip with him and it will say, April Fool's!

I know Stu so well. My friends and I will get him this time. We know his tricks. Tonight, after it gets dark, we will slip over to his house and bang on his bedroom window. We will see he is alright and playing a trick.

Carol and Brenda thought it was a great idea. So, the

three of us banged on his window about 8:00 pm. He was surprised to see us. He let us crawl through the window, and we talked and played a card game of rummy on his bed. Stu had red spots on his face. We knew he drew those on there to prove to us he was sick. We laughed, but kept the noise down, not wanting to get caught.

We left and went our separate ways. I was in my bed by nine. I couldn't wait until tomorrow to see the principal's face when he read the note that read 'April Fools'. I slept well, thinking maybe I liked Stu more than I thought I did. He was funny and fun to be around.

Next morning, I was having my breakfast when my mom noticed some small red dots on my face and then some more on my arm.

"What? What is this?" I screamed. "No, this can't be!"

Sure enough, it was. Stu had given me and my friends measles. We were sick at home for days. He was really sick. Who put that puppy in the tree? Nobody ever found out. I still think it was Stu, but then again, there might be another prankster in our midst.

Chapter 9
Good Decisions

I John 5:14   *And this is the confidence that we have in him, that, if we ask any thing according to his will, he heareth us.*

Jeremiah 33:3   *Call unto me, and I will answer thee, and show thee great and mighty things, which thou knowest not.*

James 3:17   *But the wisdom that is from above is first pure, then peaceable, gentle, and easy to be intreated, full of mercy and good fruits, without partiality, and without hypocrisy.*

Signs in the Sky

It was April 8, 2024. About 1:30 in the afternoon, Dad heard a lot of noise and excited talking coming from the back porch. He left the movie on pause to check things out.

"What's all the commotion about?"

"Dad, come see the eclipse!" Sarah handed her dad a pair of solar glasses. "Put these on first. It can blind you if you look at it without the glasses."

"Oh, okay. Move over, though. This porch is too crowded with all your friends. Why aren't they out in the yard?"

"They don't want to get hit by flying debris." Sarah flung her arm out, showing her dad the debris flying across the yard. The wind had picked up, and dirt, leaves, and small twigs were swirling everywhere.

"Oh, I see. I didn't know it was so windy."

"Yeah. The wind just started as the solar eclipse began. It's a freaky thing."

"Wow, that is interesting." Dad stood motionless, looking up at the sun as the moon crossed in front, blocking out the sunlight.

Daryl came near and handed Sarah a solar filter for

her phone. She put it on and took pictures. One after the other, catching many frames as the sunlight was blocked. It only lasted four minutes or so for the entire eclipse to begin and end.

"Wow, that was spectacular!" Daryl was ecstatic. He was still looking up even after the sun was shining brightly once more.

The other teenagers were comparing their photos. Each a little better than the others, or so they thought. Ten teenagers excited about an eclipse. Dad was surprised the younger generation enjoyed natural phenomenon.

"Come inside and have a soda," Dad said.

The teenagers rushed to the door. Sarah pulled out two bags of potato chips and placed them on the kitchen counter. Dad pulled cold drinks from the fridge. He liked seeing Sarah's friends at their house. He thought it was good to make them feel welcome. Dad could keep his eye on his daughter better if they were at their house rather than at a friend's house.

Dad excused himself to go back to watching his movie. He invited Sarah's friends to join him if they wished. Sarah seemed pleased her dad was so accommodating.

Daryl said, "Your dad is a great guy, Sarah. I wish my dad was more like him."

"Yes, he is pretty wonderful."

The teenagers finished their snack. Todd and Jeremy made their way into the living room. They sat down and watched the movie with Sarah's dad. Joni and Toni, the twins and Jerry, told Sarah goodbye. They left to go to Jerry's house.

Susan and Barbara, and Daryl, hung out for a while with Sarah. They went outside to sit and chat about the eclipse. Susan told them her pastor had talked about the eclipse in his sermon the day before. He said it was a sign in the sky from God Almighty. It was a sign of the times.

Daryl asked, "What did he mean by that?"

"He said it was prophesy, like when Jonah went to Nineveh to preach to the people there to repent of their sins."

"I heard something about there being seven towns named Nineveh that the eclipse passed through," Sarah said.

Susan agreed that was true. She said the eclipse in Jonah's day was a sign to repent or judgment was coming. The Ninevites had already seen God's judgment and knew they needed to repent. They did and their city was saved.

Barbara joined in. "Do you think this is a warning from God for us?"

"I absolutely do. My pastor does too. It is complicated, but there are many things happening with this eclipse, more than coincidence." She explained the other eclipse, the one that occurred seven years prior. The two together make an X over central Illinois, where they live. She talked about Bible prophecy and how relevant it is in today's world.

The teens sat in silence for a few minutes, pondering what was said and what had occurred. Sarah broke the silence. "I think I will ask forgiveness of all my sins right here, right now."

Everyone was surprised and looked bewildered. It did not stop Sarah. She bowed her head and began to pray aloud. "Oh Lord, my God. I know I am a sinner and have not followed your will in my life. Please forgive me. Help me to live according to your will, like the Bible tells me to do. Forgive my stubbornness and my anger and judgment towards people who do not deserve it. Help me to be a light in the world and a help to others. In Jesus' name."

The silence was deafening. Then Daryl jumped in and said, "Yes, dear Lord, me too. Everything Sarah said, let it be true for me as well. I am sorry for my sins and ask Your forgiveness. Let me become the man you will be proud of. Help me to serve You."

Barbara said, "Well, if you two can do that, so can I. Dear God, I mean Jesus. Forgive me too. I have been especially hateful to my parents lately, and I am sorry. I know I have many faults and I need help. I need Your forgiveness. I want to live for you, Jesus. Make me a child of God. I don't know how to do anything you want me to do, but I am willing to learn. Forgive me, dear God. I love you, Jesus."

Susan was so delighted. Her friends were coming to God like she had prayed for them to do for several years. "Would you all like to go meet my pastor? He can explain things better for you than I can?"

"Yes, let's go!" Sarah said, "let me tell my dad where we are going."

The teens left to go see Susan's pastor and witness to him the prayers they all prayed. He visited with them the remainder of the afternoon. The pastor gave them literature to take home, and invited them to come to church. The teens made important commitments that day. The eclipse was the beginning of a renewal of faith in the young people of this town in central Illinois. This town would never be the same!

Susan's prayers were answered that day by signs in the sky.

Finish What You Start

As Cameron walked out of the interview, there was an uneasy feeling in her spirit. The interview had gone well, and she thought she might get the job. Her answers were quick and decisive, and the interviewer seemed to like her quickness and complimented her several times on her fast observance and rationale in reaching the answers to the presented questions. However, some statements made by him made her wonder if this was the right place for her.

Teamwork was something he emphasized repeatedly. She believed in teamwork, and her past basketball experience in high school and college had prepared her in a great way to appreciate teamwork. But she wondered, was he saying something different from what she was thinking?

Was he inferring that you should 'go along to get along'? She ran the whole interview through her mind. She must think about this and understand for sure what the interviewer meant before she made her decision to work for this company, if she was chosen for the position.

Would she be chosen out of the multitude of

applicants? The job market was tough these days. There were more college graduates than jobs in her field. How could she compete when she had dropped out of school? The missing degree on her resume' told her she could not be too picky.

What did a degree mean? Did the person with a degree mean they were smarter or more capable? Did it mean they stuck it out to the very end? Would an interviewer or employer believe the degreed person was more likely to stay with the company? It had proven detrimental to her job search several times. Should she try to go back to school? How important was finishing?

Circumstances in her personal life had been tempting and caused her to not take the last semester of her degree program. She was near the end, and she had taken the hardest courses already. She had a lot of knowledge, and now she had working experience. Cameron had managed a mid-size company for a family friend. She had done a good job, but when the pandemic happened, the supply chain issues put them out of business.

It was not her fault. She had done well. Her employer was near retirement and told her he was not going to back into business and fight it any longer. The work she had done was appreciated, and she had a glowing referral letter, but was it enough?

She knew how to manage people. She knew her business, and how her skills could transfer to a different product or industry. But the degree designation, or lack thereof, was getting in the way. She knew if she landed the job without the degree, the company would automatically pay her less, even though her skills could be more than her competition.

As Cameron walked down the street, she considered all these things. Her two young children depended on her. She had a mortgage payment, car payment, utility bills, all the expenses of a household, and raising two children by herself. How could she possibly go back to school and get that dreaded degree that was holding her back?

It was a long walk to the unemployment office. That was a good thing, because she had much to consider. She knew if she landed this job, she would be working more hours and it would be for less than she had been making. It would be hard to keep up with the bills, but she could make it.

She had a big decision to make. Keep trying, hoping a better opportunity would come along during the six months she had on unemployment, or take the lesser job with a sure paycheck every week. Then, there was the possibility of going back to school and getting that degree. That would take the entire six months, and then what?

She shook her head in frustration as she signed in at the unemployment office. She told her counselor about the interview she had and her concerns about it. Her counselor was a caring woman. She listened intently, and Cameron felt there was genuine concern. So, she listened as the woman, who was constantly busy with applicants, took extra time to counsel her.

She told Cameron to go home and pray about her decision. She said, "God finishes what He starts." Cameron was surprised the woman talked to her about God, but she was glad she did. It was unusual for someone in her position, but it was great advice.

The evening was like any other: dinner, homework, playing a game, baths, and off to bed for the children. Cameron finished cleaning the kitchen and started up her computer. She had some things she needed to look up. TV movies were not for tonight. She pulled up her transcript and glanced over it. Then, looked up Pell grants. No, I can't do that, she thought. Turning everything off, she went to bed exhausted and frustrated.

Cameron spent the night in prayer. She tossed and turned in the bed, replaying the decisions she could make and what could be expected outcomes. Cameron remembered the words of the interviewer and the feeling that compromise would be a big part of her new job, if she took that position. She looked into the possibility of a Pell grant to go back to college to get her degree before she went to bed. What she read on the internet was optimistic.

There was so much to consider. She had to make the right decision. She could not mess up this time. Her children depended on her, and there was no one else she could lean on. The money had to come in and she had to make it.

She remembered her dad. He told her, "Always finish what you start." It didn't seem to matter that much when he reminded her of those words when she left college early to get married. Her husband had his career in full swing, and money was not lacking then. If only she had listened to her dad. He had the wisdom she needed now. But his counselling passed, when he died a few years ago.

Mom had been gone for a while, and dad became her best friend after her husband found a younger, richer, new wife. They had moved far away. The absent father syndrome was probably better for her kids, since his lack of attention seemed to hurt more than not being around. Why had she expected him to be like her dad? She had made a grave mistake marrying such a man, and now, she could not make another grave mistake. A mistake like that could affect her and her children's lives for a long time. She needed her dad to talk to.

Remembering what the unemployment office counsellor said about praying, she got out of bed and on her knees. Closing her eyes, she said in a whisper, "Hey Lord. Remember me?" The tears flowed down her cheeks. It had been too long since she prayed, at least a real prayer. Sure, there were dinner time prayers like a few seconds saying a repeated phrase. But now she was on her knees. This was real. This was serious.

Clearing her throat, she started again. "Dear God, I need your help. I can no longer figure things out for myself. Things are hard, and I have nobody else to talk to. Please talk to me, dear Jesus. I need you, Lord." She sniffled and wiped her nose.

"Lord, I don't want to make another mistake by not listening. Dad said to always pray and listen to you. I'm not sure how to hear your voice. Please hear me though, God. Please answer my prayer in a way I can understand it is you talking to me. Dad told me I will have peace in my heart when I make the right decision. He said it comes from you. Peace comes from you."

Cameron continued to talk to God. She cried and cried, and then prayed and cried some more. She was exhausted when she finally just stretched out on the floor and went to sleep. As she dreamed, the words her dad spoke to her came back to the top of her mind. "God always finishes what He starts."

After one hour, she awoke mouthing the words of her dream. "God always finishes what He starts." She said it again out loud. Smiling and rising from the floor, she knew what she needed to do.

She went to her computer and filled out the

application for the Pell grant. She would finish her college degree. If she needed a part-time job, she would do whatever she had to do to make ends meet. She would not let not having that degree hold her back any longer. She would teach her children that finishing what you start is the way to success.

Cameron would be the example of doing what you say you will do. She would show the world a single parent can make it, if you are willing to do the hard work. Being the example to her children, that her dad was to her, was worth the extra effort. She knew her dad would be proud of the decision she had made. God was proud, too. She knew it because of the peace she had in her heart.

The Cards You Are Dealt

"Not everybody is given a beautiful life, Missy! You play the cards you have been dealt." As the old gambler walked away, I could detect a slight limp on his left side. I wondered if it was caused by the knifing he endured years ago. I had heard the story many times from the shoe shine boy on the corner.

Shoe shine boy looked up to the gambler. He loved shining his boots because the gambler always tipped him a bright, new, shiny silver dollar. Shoe shine boy told me he had a whole jar of those silver dollars and that he would never spend them. He was saving them to go to college one day. He said he would not be shining shoes for the rest of his life. I believed he would meet his goals. Shoe shine boy had a determination that nothing would be out of his reach.

The gambler told Missy she must play the cards she had been dealt. I am sure he had told shoe shine boy the same thing. Would Missy be determined to change her life like shoe shine boy? I didn't know if she had the same fortitude, but I imagined if gambler told her long enough, something would rise up inside her.

I sold papers up and down the street. Gambler had made an impression on me, and I knew I would not always be doing this. I was going to be a reporter one day. An investigative reporter, one that digs up the news, discovers things others cannot. That was me. I was made for a job like that. People might think I'm just a poor paper girl, selling newspapers one at a time to get by.

People underestimate me. I am smart, and I will use my brain instead of my body to learn a trade that will take me places I want to go. Sure, the gambler has said those same words to me. They made an impression. When I am old like him, I hope to have affected many lives for the better. It's hard to think an old gambler did something so good for me, but he did. You never know where good advice may come from. So, I take it all in, and weigh it. I keep some, and I throw the rest away. A smart person gleans the good and discards the bad.

I wonder what Missy will do?

Missy lives with her alcoholic father. Her mother died three years ago from cancer. She does all the housework now and cooks the evening meal. Missy is a good student, but she has a boyfriend that is nothing but trouble. Why she would pick someone like that to hang out with is beyond my imagination. Darren skips school regularly and I am sure he has tried to get Missy to do the same. So far, she is more afraid of her father than of skipping school.

Whenever I work late, I see Darren hanging around outside her house, trying to get a look at Missy through her windows. I have even caught them talking through her bedroom window late at night. She is headed for trouble if she keeps talking to him. I want to tell her, but she would just get angry with me. She might even think I was trying to break them up so I could have Darren. Nothing would be further from the truth. I can't stand him. His attitude is the opposite of someone I would want. Besides, I am working toward my career. I will find someone to share my life with after I am fully grown and making it on my own.

*****

Fourteen years have passed since I walked these streets. It feels good to come back here and look around at the old neighborhood. I have my dream job. I am an investigative reporter, and my assignment today is flushing out the facts of the murder of an old gentleman that wore cowboy boots and a felt cowboy hat. He was always dressed nice and flipped a silver dollar as he strolled down the street with total confidence. He made many friends, and he made many enemies. Apparently, one of his enemies unloaded a gun in his belly last night.

The suspect was caught and charged with his murder, but the suspect is the son of the district attorney. My boss thought this had the makings of a good story and thought many details might be left out. Therefore, he sent his best reporter to flush out the facts. That's me.

Why would the son of the district attorney be filled with so much hate for this old gambler? It sounds like he got a bad deal.

I am anxious to find out what happened to my old friends. Missy and her boyfriend, Darren, got married, I am told. She has a brood of kids, and Darren, like her father, is an alcoholic. She played the cards she was dealt, but she didn't win.

I hear shoe shine boy made it big. He graduated from college and is now a U.S. senator. He had more gumption than me. I am proud of him, and I voted for him in the last election. He had some bad cards too, but he threw those back in the pile and kept the good ones. He drew a few more good ones, and his hand was a winning one.

I remember the old gambler saying; we play the hand we are dealt. We do, but we can make changes if we don't like that hand. I made changes and am better for it. I will investigate this murder, write a story, and move on. I live in a better place today, because I knew what to keep and what to throw away.

The Best Decision I Ever Made

What can a smile do? A simple hello, how are you doing today? Can touch someone like it touched me that day. It was the Spring of 1968. My husband and I went to a Sunday morning service at a nearby church we had driven by several times. We knew no one that went there, and we were not invited. But we went anyway.

We wanted a church family. Being new to the area, we needed to meet some people, and going to church seemed like the right thing to do. I was three months pregnant, and I wanted to raise my children in church.

My parents did not go to church or talk about God. It was a foreign thing in our household while I was growing up. I had decided early in life, my family would be different. I watched my favorite teachers in school and knew about their church attendance. It motivated me to want the same for my family.

Now that I was about to be a new mother, it was even more important. I shared my feelings with my husband, and he agreed. We would find a place to worship and raise our children in a Christian home.

There was only one problem. I didn't know how to

become a Christian. Would I be a Christian if I joined a church? Maybe that's it. I would go and find out.

That first Sunday morning was delightful. Many people shook our hands and welcomed us. The singing was great, even though I didn't know the songs. It was easy to follow along with the hymnals. My foot was tapping to the fast songs, and a smile was on my face. Joy was springing up in my soul, and it felt so good.

The preaching was good. It sounded like the preacher knew what he was talking about. He read from the Bible, something I had never done before. Sure, we had bibles in our home when I was young. They sat on the bookshelf, never being opened once while I lived with my parents. My job was dusting, so they got dusted occasionally. Touching one was not going to hurt me. I wanted to know God, and know more about Him.

My mom gave me one from her bookshelf several months before all this. It was in my home now, if I ever wanted to read it. Up to this point, I truly had not given it a thought. But listening to the preacher, I thought I might open it when I got home.

When the service was over, many came and introduced themselves and shook our hands. Then they shook hands with the preacher and left. We were some of the last to leave because we were talking to our new acquaintances.

The last person to reach her hand out to shake mine

was an elderly lady named Mrs. Lord. She was frail and stood shorter than me. Her solid gray hair glistened. Her wrinkled face had the warmest smile as she held my hand in hers. I connected.

Her big brown eyes were soft and deep. They penetrated my soul. The aura of God surrounded her little frame. My heart melted as she looked deep inside my being, reading my questions that had never been asked. I felt she knew my most personal thoughts and feelings.

Mrs. Lord didn't need to converse mighty words. Her love poured out like overflowing water, bathing my soul in Godly love I'd never known. Finally, she spoke, and asked us to come back on Wednesday night. Without thinking, I immediately said we would. That simple invitation would change my life.

Mrs. Lord was there on Wednesday night. She met me at the door and welcomed my husband and me inside. I had never been to a Wednesday night service. It started out a lot the same as the Sunday service. There was singing and prayers. Then, the preacher said a few words and asked if anyone in the congregation had a testimony.

A testimony? What was that? I sat still and quiet and just listened. A middle-aged lady jumped up and started sharing about her life, and when she met the Lord. Met the Lord? I wondered what she meant.

When she sat down, a man behind her stood up and talked about meeting Jesus. Meeting Jesus? Again, I didn't understand. I listened closely. Surely, these people knew something I didn't know. Have they really met God? Do they know Jesus Christ personally?

One by one, they stood and testified. I learned the meaning of the words that Wednesday night. Mrs. Lord was one of the last to stand and testify. She talked about meeting Jesus when she was a young girl. Her recollections were vivid, just like it happened yesterday. She was born in the late 1800s and received Christ before the turn of the century. Mrs. Lord was really old, but she had the sparkle in her eyes that only God can put there.

She was the most interesting person I had ever known. I wanted to be around her more and learn from her.

To my surprise, everyone in the church had stood and testified of their love for our Savior and Lord, except for my husband and me. Then the preacher said, "Is there anyone else?"

I was shocked when my husband stood up and told everyone about going to a Campus Crusade for Christ meeting when he was eleven years old. He had accepted Jesus at the time, but his parents refused to allow him to be baptized. We had never discussed anything like this. I sat paralyzed. I was the only one in the whole church that could not stand and say I had accepted Jesus as my personal Savior and Lord.

I had wanted to know how to be saved for years. I prayed often, but I didn't know how to be saved. Now, it had been revealed to me through these precious saints of God. Listening to Billy Graham on television give invitations to meet Jesus was confusing. I did not understand the terminology of receiving Christ. How do you receive Christ?

After hearing these adults confess their sins, give God glory and praise, and speak about asking Jesus to save them and give them a home in heaven, I knew. I finally knew. It is a simple prayer of confessing sins, and receiving the forgiveness Jesus gives. Asking and believing is all it is. Jesus has done the work on the cross, a sacrifice for our sins because He loves us.

We just acknowledge his gift of grace and mercy and take the gift He is giving, and commit our lives to Him.

On the way home that night, I looked up into the sky. It was very dark, but the stars were twinkling as we topped the hill. I felt closer to heaven than ever before. I said, "Jesus, forgive me of my sins, and come live in my heart and life. I receive You as my Savior and Lord, and I give my life to You. I will follow You all the days of my life."

I was saved at that moment. I knew it by the peace I had. When I got home, I opened my Bible and began to learn of God's love for me. The next Wednesday I stood and testified. I made my confession before men and women. That sealed my salvation. I was a new Christian and my family would be raised in church. Our baptisms came a month later.

I am so glad I belong to Jesus. It is the best decision I have ever made. I love Him more every day, and I look forward to my eternal home in heaven.

Mrs. Lord

***Excerpt from:* The Best Decision I Ever Made**

Her big brown eyes were soft and deep. They penetrated my soul. The aura of God surrounded her little frame. My heart melted as she looked deep inside my being, reading my questions that had never been asked. I felt she knew my most personal thoughts and feelings.

Mrs. Lord didn't need to converse mighty words. Her love poured out like overflowing water bathing my soul in Godly love I'd never known.

Mrs. Lord was a lady I once knew,
With a heart of love that grew and grew.
Her big brown eyes could pierce your soul,
Fill your heart, until it could not hold.

The love that flowed from this dear one,
Until her life on earth was done.
Immeasurable love, just like God,
Nothing like it, it was totally odd.

I loved her more than she knew,
Her love for me, made me new.
Her faith was real, and it showed,
Jesus is mine now, that's how I know.

Jesus, my Jesus

Jesus, my Jesus, how I love you.
There is no other One like you.
Jesus, my Jesus, I love you,
May my heart ever be true.

Never apart from me,
With me, you'll always be.
My life, my breath, my thoughts, my love.
Is only You and heaven above.

Never dark, only light,
Daily as the years go by.
You are the only One I need,
You are all I want to see.

I lean on You, more of the time.
I am a branch, You are the vine.
Giving me life for each new day,
Helping me know what to say.

I am yours, and You are mine,
Singing songs and making rhyme.
Jesus, my Jesus, I love you so,
How wonderful You are, all must know.

Letter to my Readers

Thank you for reading **Tickle Me With Love**. I hope you enjoyed it, and it lifted your spirit and gave you a chuckle now and then. Entertainment that refreshes your soul is important to me, and God has given me the opportunity to make people smile inside their hearts. I count myself privileged to entertain you for a short while with my short stories and poems.

I also hope you have been encouraged. If life gets you down, remember tomorrow is another day, and the Lord is waiting to lift you out of despair. I could never have made it this far in life without my faith in Jesus. He has sustained me when nobody else was there. He will do the same for you.

If you liked my book, please take time to rate the book and write a review on Amazon. This is the way people find new authors. I would be so appreciative. As an Indie author, I am blessed to have your time and attention to this matter. Tell your friends about my books, so I can continue to try to entertain and uplift others.

Thank you so much for being one of my readers. You can find all my books on Amazon or on my website in paperback or e-book, and some in audible. Www.RickiMcCallumBooks.com or www.castnetpress.com. You will find interesting articles on my blog also located there. Reach out to me anytime from my website. Thank you again.

The End Is Just the Beginning

It's always hard to say Goodbye,
Grandpa Tom told me as I said "Hi."
Our visits were all so sweet,
Talking for hours, Grandpa and me.

His great big smile warmed my heart,
Holding my hand, never wanting to part.
Grandpa was a kind man above all,
Big in my eyes, in stature rather small.

No one can take his place,
The hole he left came in haste.
No, he cannot be gone from this world,
Crying, sobbing, my head in a whirl.

Then, I remembered what he said,
"Until we meet again," filled my head.
"See you again in heaven up there,
Never fall for the devil's snare.

May Jesus keep you, my special one,
I'll love you forever until it's done.
We'll be together before too long,
Hearts of joy, singing a song.

My granddaughter, never lose hope,
Jesus is coming again, so please don't mope.
I'll be with Him when He comes,
On a white horse, shining like the sun."

Time has passed and I long to see him once more,
My Grandpa and me walking through the same door.
It's a gate made of a giant pearl,
Now I'm a woman, not a little girl.

Will he recognize me after all this time?
I'm an author of stories and books of rhyme.
Grandpa, it is me, I say,
Together again, what a wonderful day!

The End

Acknowledgements

Every writer has many people in their lives that deserve thanks and recognition. My husband helps me proof and edit my books, and I am thankful for the time and attention he gives to this purpose. Thank you, Harold McCallum.

I have many author friends that also give me their time and advice on various projects. My author friend, Judy Harrington is one such special person. Her support for me has been invaluable, and I thank her. Our fun times with book signings and events have added to our friendship. I wrote the poem Author to Author about her and me. She loved it.

There are several writer's groups I belong to, and each person there adds to my knowledge and understanding of this writing craft. Thank you all! It is a journey every writer makes. We grow and learn together along the way. I hope I never stop learning, and that my writing continues to improve and please my reader audience.

Special thanks to Aaron Ray for outstanding covers for this book and four others. He is the best!

Thank you to Stein Liland and Pexels for the beautiful photo of the northern lights that helped produce an excellent cover.

Thank you to R.M. Snider, writer, author, editor, and friend. You are always helpful and so appreciated!